ARRIVAL PRESS

A TASTE OF THE NORTH

Edited

By

TRUDI PURDY

First published in Great Britain in 1993 by
ARRIVAL PRESS
1 - 2 Wainman Road, Woodston,
Peterborough, PE2 7BU

All Rights Reserved

Copyright Contributors 1993

Foreword

Welcome to the second Arrival Press Northern anthology. I hope that this year's offering will be as successful, if not more so, than the previous one. The poems included depict a certain group of counties. The work in this book is about the North.

Writers from all walks of life have come together to express their thoughts and feelings to concoct this poetical guide to the North. Aspects of their innermost views on their home towns and counties are penned with depth, provoking a real insight into their cultural and traditional way of life.

Reading through this anthology will open a window into the area of the country that the poets included come from, giving you a fresh breath of their lives.

If you get the same enjoyment out of reading this book as I did from helping to compile it, then it will be a delight to return to again and again.

Michelle Abbott
Assistant Editor

Contents

The Yorkshire Coast	E Lawrence	1
An Invitation	Dorothy Ashby	2
It's Tradition you See	Ruth Wolstenholme	3
Yorkshire	C Ross	4
Bolton Priory	Nora Morgan	5
Pennine Farm	Denis Golby	6
The Dales Surprise	C Potter	7
I've Travelled Far	Hazel P Marsay	8
Whitby	Elizabeth Haines	9
Beautiful Dales	S Poore	10
Saltburn by the Sea	Audrey Golby	11
Beloved Wolds	Pamela Pitts	12
Spring Call	S Duckworth	13
Tribute to the Soldier	David Smith	14
Morning Campers	Victoria Waller	15
Northern Changes	Monique Richardson	16
May Night above Cray	J D Riddiough	17
Stupid Young Mugs	Stephen Rattigan	18
The Angler	H Davis	19
Everyone	Trevor Berry	20
Magical York	Kathleen Rudd	21
Homeland	Marie Hirst	22
The Sea	Sarah Louise Wood	23
Six Directions	M D Hollingworth	24
A Sheffield Evening	John Critchley	26
Welcome	Madge Parker	27
Huddersfield Love	G A Jones	28
My Yorkshire	G W Scotrick	29
Penine View	Betty Walton	30
My Yorkshire	Hilda Kaye Gibson	31
Yorkshire	Muriel Rodgers	32
Its Name is Progress	Lyndis M Winterbottom	33
Betrayal	Anne P Robbins	34
Snow on Yorkshire Moors	Elizabeth Newell	35
Ginnie Lane	Kathleen Pogson	36
My Yorkshire	Audrey Drake	37

Title	Author	Page
Yorkshire	Glenda Lawrence	38
I Had a View	R Lewis	39
The Stare	John Earwaker	40
Hill Farm - Reluctant Sale - Divorce Pending	Fay Blackburn	41
Unfertile Hopes	K Casewell	42
Jewel of the North	Lena Doherty	43
The Countryside	F Taylor	44
Crimsworth Dean Chapel	Fay Fielding	45
A Pennine Dawning	Anne Penney	46
Green Gowns	Brian Gregan	47
The Yorkshire Dales	Mike Arrowsmith	48
The North	S Winder	49
Sheffield Parkway	Mags Wigram	50
Yorkshire Pride	A Bellingham	51
Cold Doncaster	B V Walker	52
Ode for the Ball and Chainers	Marilyn Drozd	53
Words to Remedy Homesickness	Kathryn M Horner	54
High Pennines	E R Groves	55
Black Diamonds	Hazel Collins	56
Yorkshire	M Sunderland	57
England's North Land	K B Lambert	59
Cock O the North	Mary Fardell	60
Textiles	L Mansfield	61
My Old Man Keeps Pigeons	Mary P Linney	62
Dales	Mary Hodgson	63
My City	B Elliott	64
A Northern Morn	Mark Hudson	65
The Statis Fun-Fair	Barry Porter	66
A Scot in Yorkshire	Nora Knox	67
Far off Church Bells	Stuart Alan Wroe	68
A Yorkshireman's Dream	Helen Fardell	69
Yorkshire's Pride	Eric Langford	70
Yorkshire Life	Joanne Jowitt	71
My Country My Home	Christine Johnson	72
Wordminer	Neil Fletcher	73
Northern Lands	Denise Frost	74

Pictures - in my Mind	Val Wilkinson	75
Tramps	Malcolm Freedman	76
Thoughts on North York Moors	Josephine S White	77
Tadcaster Town	B Harrison	78
Motherland	Neil White	79
The County Fair	D Bagshaw	81
Reflections	Nan Bickford	82
North Country Birds	Margaret Lumb	83
Jam Jars of Delight	Cynthia Howe	84
Beloved View	B E Marsden	85
Septic Cut	Tommy McLoughlin	86
Memories of Autumn	Steve McDool	87
East Yorkshire Man's Dilemma	Ron Grantham	88
Scarborough Then and Now	Derek Colville	89
A Miner's Lament	Anne Dawes	90
Penned on the Pennines	Marguerite C Guile	91
The Historic Town	Anne Stocks	92
Crummockdale in June	Joan Smith	93
Rain	Pat Mason	94
Four Seasons	R A Fenwick	95
The Deserted Village	Margaret Throup Lancaster	96
Huddersfield my Town	Jane Elizabeth Williams	97
Yorkshire Pride	M Ward	98
Why?	Margaret R Sayers	99
Ode to Almscliffe Crag	Gladys Mallinson	100
Fed Up	T Broadbent	101
In a Northern Hospice	Krystyna Lejk	102
In Harmony	J Dejongh	103
The White Rose	Penny Batchelor	104
Four Seasons	David Clark	105
Sheffield - My Home	Vera Percy	106
A Visit to the Summer Exhibition	Geraldine Outhwaite	107
Twixt Lancashire and Yorkshire	Mary Chadwick	108
The Visionary	Claire Collins	109
My Home Town	M M Walker	110
Lakeland	John Potter	111

Scunthorpe v Rotherham	Lesley Marshall	112
The Fallen Empire	Ben Stone	114
Cleethorpes	Jane Marriott	116
The Scarborough School	Mavis Hall	118
Waterbaby	Christine Ross	119
Yorkshiremen are Barmy	Steve Sheppard	120
The North	Lorna Montaque	122
The Last Bus Stop	Pete Haythorne	123
Doncaster	M E Lavin	124
Conisborough Castle	Gwen Bedford	125
The Voice of Micklefield	Dennis Best	126
Yorkshire Images	Vera Hansson	127
All Rounder	Keith Jenkinson	128
Three Haiku From the Dales	Marion Sinton	129
Second Childhood	Doris Wilkinson	130
The Pigeon Fancier	Elisabeth Barlow	131
Sonnet to Lakeland's Autumn Loveliness	Christopher R Shaw	132
Up Beyond Moor Lane	Martin Dutton	133
Our Lovely Yorkshire Moor	Mannah McAndrew	134
Yorkshire Born	Dorothy Mason	135
Ingleborough Contrast	I Taylor	136
Returning to Flamborough Head	Jim Hart	137
Poetry of the North	P Watson	138
Yorkshire Talk	Jim Armstrong	139
Springtime	Jean Foster	140
Shrovetide Fiesta	Florence Needler	141
The Humber Forts	Ray Waugh	142
Unemployment	Edna Watford Harvey	143
Home	Hazel Jackson	144
Untitled	Edith Norris	145
To Otley Chevin	Kathleen Padbury	146
Robin Hood's Bay	Christine Lee	147
Super Tram	Tricia Mead	148
My Place	Julia A Smith	149
An Exile's Dream of Home	Kathleen Roelich	150
Progress	B Lenson	151

Robin Hood's Bay	David Kennedy	152
Home Sweet Home	Denny Rhymer	153
Where Does Time Go?	Andrew Frith	154

The Yorkshire Coast

Come to the vanishing coastline, before it fades away,
To Filey with its jutting Brigg, and loud and thunderous spray.
Yet Fishermen still go to sea, in cobbles they go out,
While Flamborough Head's big lighthouse, shines on them from the
south,
On to Bempton you must go, 300 ft cliffs of chalk.
In the spring reward is great, for that cliff top walk.
For a breeding colony of Gannets, and other birds there's lots.
Razorbill and puffins and lovely guillemots.

Bridlington, old world resort, with safe and sandy beaches.
Safely guarded by the bay, out of rough sea's reaches,
South from here a lovely coast, the playground of the bay,
There even is seclusion, with naturalists at play.
Further down along the coast, we come to Hornsea Mere
A hugh lake of fresh water is situated here.

Cormarants and Heron, come here to raise their young,
But just a mile away the sea's erosion has begun,
Mapleton was nearly gone, almost to its Spier,
Luckily then man stepped in and made defences higher.
Cowden next beyond repair, there's not much left to see.
Where there was a village, there's half a mile of sea.

As we go along the coast through Holderness to Spurn,
A slip of land and beaches with hardly room to turn,
A group of little cottages, for lifeboat men to be,
Many times they're cut off by the restless sea,
Here again there's refuge and solitude and peace
For birds who have migrated and flown from south and east,
Waders stocking up once more, and Terns they dive in splendour,
The Yorkshire coast's a lovely place you always will remember.

E Lawrence

An Invitation

Travel to Doncaster and you will find
A town of a cosmopolitan kind,
A racecourse of St. Leger fame
A Dome for leisure - Name the game?
A market, nation-wide renowned
Where value is gained for every pound,
Our shopping centre will delight,
The discerning spender with only a mite,
A Mansion House in the centre of town
Where Councillors meet to vote the countdown,
Places of interest and history
Are found in villages of notoriety,
See Epworth of John Wesley's time,
Showing memorabilia of his prime,
The Pilgrim Fathers left from Scrooby,
A coaching Inn named *The Crown* at Bawtry,
Antiquities at Cusworth Hall,
Take tea and cakes that will enthral,
Sprotborough lies beside the river
There Walter Scott made his mark forever,
In a little house near the rush of the falls,
He wrote *Ivanhoe* to thrill one and all,
Remember Stirling and the age of steam?
Loco works where engines gleam.
Take a train - a mainline link
With London, Glasgow and coastline brink.
Paris will soon be accessible too.
So why not make us your rendezvous?
We were once called *poor, proud and pretty*
Our very next aim is to become a city!

Dorothy Ashby

It's Tradition you See

Yorkshire and proud of it
We're hard nuts to crack
And we're tough as steel.
But with hearts that are tender
like true Scouts
We believe in good deeds
It's tradition you see.

We live for sport, it's in our Blood
A big cheer goes up
When our Cricketers win
Our faces light up
With a perpetual grin
It's tradition you see.

I'm from Yorkshire
So were my parents
and Grandparents before me
We can go back centuries ago
We are proud of the fact.

We've been brought up, on Stew and Dumplings
Roast Beef, and good old Yorkshire Pudding
Me Mam, she liked a glass of Owd Ale
and a slice of Spice Cake
Yes! we're true Yorkshire people
We're proud of the fact
It's tradition you see.

Ruth Wolstenholme

Yorkshire

We had North, East, and West riding,
Alas all have gone into hiding,
We now have Yorkshire North, South and West,
But the largest county is still the best,
Tourists visit the Minster at York,
Drive to the moors, take a walk,
Our cricket has lately gone down the swanee,
But the state of soccer, and rugby, look bonny,
Oh those days when kids played taws,
Gathered heather on the moors,
Little girls playing hopscotch and skipping,
Giving their tops plenty of whipping,
We played kick-out-can and leap frog,
Didn't bother about rain, snow or smog,
Yes, Yorkshire is England's best county 't would seem,
We've had visits from Royalty, even the Queen,
We end by saying, we've great Cities, Moors and the Dales,
And not least of all Mother Skipton's tales,
I'll add a PS about Yorkshire Pud,
It's not only tasty it does you good!

C Ross

Bolton Priory

I came to Yorkshire's windswept moors,
The hills and Dales enthralled me.
Each had it's beck and little falls
Or wider, swirling river.
So varied in their wild terrain,
Their habitat just swarming
With nature's wonder manifest.
The curlew cry, the black faced sheep
That graze amongst the cotton grass,
All new to my experience.
Then came the time that we must leave
And drive, between the drystone walls
That line the lanes and climb the hills.
For miles until, quite suddenly,
We stopped and knew that we had found
Foundations of a Priory.
We still had endless miles to go,
And as it seemed all ruins,
We just admired the mellowed stone,
In such a perfect setting.
The years passed by - some twenty odd -
Then I returned to Yorkshire
And found this isolated church,
A place of sacred splendour -
A restored Bolton Priory Church
Surrounded by the ruins.

Nora Morgan

Pennine Farm

The door hangs broken-jawed
by one rust-eaten hinge;
the windows are blind;
no life breathes from the stack;
no child cries in the low grey farm
hugging the hill on the high moor's edge.

Uncounted winters have clamped
beam and stone in a frozen vice
since this was last a home.
Yet so it was. Here life,
pulsing and warm, brutal and kind,
moved round a glowing hearth.

A man of Dales' upland stock
with farming in his blood
dared tame this wild moor,
bending his bitten flesh and bone
up here beyond Malham Tarn
against the Pennine wind and stone -
a grinding, unremitting toil,
alone, but for his own -
and all the world a foreigner.

Who last came through this door,
his home upon his back?
Did he close it at the last
or leave it wide to let the winter in?
At the bend of the lonely track -
the long green lane
between broken dry-stonewalls
down to another world -
did he look back?

Denis Golby

The Dales Surprise

Walls meandering
As so many foolish sheep
Rush here and there
In constant stream.
Echoing the rocks,
Tripping over limestone
Flowery pavement
Covering nature's surprises -
A perfect treasure store
Of wonder
Stretching generation
Before generation
To Centurions
Who surprised
By this landscape
Proclaimed
Their power
Only to find
That once again
Natured ruled supreme.

C Potter

I've Travelled Far

I've travelled far, I've seen the World,
I've had my fill of roaming
I've seen the mighty pyramids,
And I've dallied in the Gloaming.

I've sailed the sea, in a liner,
I've flown to the City of Rome,
But to me there's nothing finer,
Than flying right back home.

To the sheep and shepherds, on the hillside,
To the mists and the heather on the moors,
To the poppies so red, nodding gaily,
To have a talk, with old Farmer Joe.

To wander round the Stately Homes of Yorkshire,
To visit Staithes and Whitby is my dream,
To look out to the sea, from Scarborough Harbour,
Watch the moonlight on the water, as it gleams,

You can keep all your, airy-fairy places,
Your boulevards and golden miles,
Just give me a rainy day in Yorkshire,
And I'll watch the water, splashing off the tiles.

Hazel P Marsay

Whitby

Stone arms reach out to the wide North Sea
Welcoming the fishing boats
To where wind-burnt men unpack the catch
And spread the nets.
The white pewed church sits squarely in the graveyard
Where tombstones tell of shipwrecked lives.
Steep steps, worn down by many feet,
Lead to a huddle of red roofed cottages
Where the drift of kipper smoke
Is acrid in the nostrils.
Through narrow streets, across the bridge,
Up to the headland,
Where the bleached jawbones of the dead leviathan
Echo the dark skeleton of the great Abbey opposite,
On to where Captain Cook still gazes out to sea
As when a boy he watched the sailing ships
And dreamed of distant lands.

Elizabeth Haines

Beautiful Dales

Where on earth can you find such beauty rare
As the Yorkshire Dales of wonder?
Such majesty in every one, it's not possible to bare
Of panorama, that even the wind cannot put asunder
There's Swaledale, Wharfdale, Airedale, where rivers flow
Wensleydale with hills and vale, oft times covered in snow
Billowing white clouds o'er caves and caverns
One can travel the world yet not find
So many wonders of creation, the many varied kinds
There's hamlets and villages everywhere
Profusion of blooms, tendered with loving care
birds on the wing that tell of spring,
Farms abound in plenty, winding roads, stone-built fences
Air so pure, it fills the senses
Glorious Abbeys so very old
Castles that tell when knights were bold.
Lake so fair, like Windermere
Just think of the things to seek for
Pot-holes Asgarth falls, the memory will recall
All these wonders of nature so rare
Bronte country, wild yet free
Has it's place in History, but!
The Yorkshire Dales have everything, that will bring you nearer to
                                                                  God
Perhaps if quiet, the Angels will sing, this jewel of Heaven can be
                                                                   trod.

S Poore

Saltburn by the Sea

The child in blazer and Panama
gripped the donkey with her knees.
Every year she chose the grey one,
not liking change.

In the resort the streets had jewel names;
Garnet, Pearl, Coral and Diamond.
They always stayed at the same house;
familiarity was all.

The beach hut's sand rasped the floor,
the heat-rotted striped canvas,
the cliff lift and the ices -
all summer's magic.

Paddling out, braving the tide,
watched by deck-chaired relatives,
she peered into the depths
looking for shells.

Something dark and heavy washed in -
the bloated body of a sailor.
At once the sun went out;
fear had arrived.

Audrey Golby

Beloved Wolds

In contradiction to a weather prediction rain has ceased.
The sun emerges pulsing with heat.
Your age and sterness melt like a chocolate fireguard.
Your questions still hang uneasy 'What d'you say lass, shall we
chance it? A run out to the old place?'

With a flask of tea and our picnic hamper,
I float again on a tide of dreams,
Lying on grasses of sun-baked meadows,
In contract to fresh homes of glass-splintered scenes.
Wild-roses straggling like barbed-wire fences,
And nature's bright smile of the sun's celandine.
Pendant boughs ladened with soft pussy-willows,
Silvered wands gentle as angels' dawn pillows,
Clumps of primroses calling, springtime.
Mice holes and mole hills, the glimpse of a skylark,
Honey-sweet days filled with lavender, and thyme.
Translucent notes of the nightingale's repertoire,
Dewy, damp hedgerows more potent than wine.

Then back home reality guts us so cruelly
Once more we've been victims of a burglary.

Pamela Pitts

Spring Call

A long long night, with restless sleep,
but body warm from head to feet,
with trapped, but welcome body heat.
Reality seeping through hazy brain,
the constant pitter patter on window pane,
proclaiming loudly of rain again,
The vacant pillow beside my face,
just emptiness holds my embrace,
this loneliness, this solitary place.
Then the heating invades the icy room,
and daylight replaces the early gloom,
it's time to rise, the day resume.
But too quick to feel this January morn,
the sharpness of the winter thorn,
and long for a spring, not yet born,
a spring where nature displays her skill,
creating life, not destroy, or kill,
the beauty of the tulip, and the daffodil.
The miracle of the transformation,
trees then alive with bud inflation,
after their winter, windswept hibernation.
The countryside begins to thrive,
parks and gardens spring alive,
it's good to live, feel love, survive.
My changing outlook condescends,
as springtime's waiting arms extend,
Inviting, waiting, around life's bend.

S Duckworth

Tribute to the Soldier

They were young lads from Rotherham
Went to war one day, how proud they
looked as they marched away
To lands they had never seen, amongst
the lads the 5th did march the TA
Volunteers, some came back and some
did stay in graves dug for the brave.
Monuments were erected to mark their
names with pride. Also hearts were
saddened for people that had died,
Their names shall never be forgotten
their graves are there to stay, for everyone
to be reminded of lives that were given
that day.

David Smith

Morning Campers

Morning campers,
rise and shine.
Pool is freezing,
weather's fine.
Seven-thirty
Breakfast call.
Greasy fry-up,
in the hall.
Fun and games,
after dinner.
Plastic trophy,
for the winner.
Back here troops,
at end of day.
Buffet, drinks,
and cabaret.
Any questions?
No joking!
No suggestions,
and no smoking.
Seventeen hundred,
meet back here.
No strong liquor,
no draught beer.
Have fun campers,
off you go.
Hi-de-hi!
Ho-de-ho!

Victoria Waller

Northern Changes

What's happened to those cobbled streets,
And the gas lights that shone so dim.
Where's the smoke that bellowed out the factory chimney,
And sent to sulphur in.

Where children played on every path,
Bagatelle, hop skotch, whipping tops,
They had enjoyment and pleasure throughout the day,
When did this all stop.

Now the smog has all but gone,
The factories and foundries have all but shut.
And one by one the mines are closing,
I preferred the times when there wasn't much.

I miss those warm, soothing fires,
And for the coal down the path you'd traipse.
You'd fiddle and meddle in the cold dark nights,
And back in the house, black coal dust struck upon your face.

You see when I was young, that was then,
But things have come to pass,
And still throughout the day,
I see children and adults laugh.

For this is now and although years later,
Things haven't changed that much,
Except when the old memories keep creeping back,
And a tender part they touch.

Now these times are filled with progress,
And in this Northern Town I was born,
But how I love to walk those old empty streets,
with my family on my arm.

Monique Richardson

May Night above Cray

Through evening hours of long May light I stay
To breathe a purer air, limpid and cool.
Ice-blue the southern sky -
Whilst lowering clouds of grey enshroud the Pike,
Dark velvet cushions dampening out the hills,
Contrasts of form and shade.

Splash of falling water rings across the dale,
Persistent becks from countless hidden gills,
Accompanied now and then by plaintive calls,
Young lambs unsure yet of their whereabouts.
The acrobatic lapwings twist their evening flight
Against the age-old backdrop of the folded fields,
Criss-crossed and patterned by their man-made walls.
And then a peewit cries a curfew note.

Now clouds have piled in thunderous banks against the fells,
But still the twilight of this last May day is loth to fade.
A black-faced ewe, breath rising in the cold night air,
Looks on, dugs butted roughly by her suckling lamb.
She too must sense a deepening silence over all,
Save for that endless business of tumbling streams
Which lull the hills to sleep.

J D Riddiough

Stupid Young Mugs

Stupid young mugs
on drink and hard drugs
wheeling and dealing
scrounging and stealing
smoking the weed
going to seed
hanging round bars
thieving from cars
smelly and dirty
braindead by thirty.

Stephen Rattigan

The Angler

There's a lot to be said for fishing
Or the piscatorial arts.
It's more peaceful than being in the boozer
And playing at cards or darts.

It's more skilful than watching the telly
Or bowls on a nice summer's day.
But most fish are real wily creatures,
To the angler they're not easy prey.

But fishing today is advancing
We must all meet the technical term.
For now they use gozzers and casters
In place of the old fashioned worm.

Zoomers, stick floats and wagglers
Replaced the old crow quill float.
Swimfeeders revolutionised baiting
And that brings a lump to my throat.

Electronic detectors and patented baits
Don't give the fish much of a chance.
But as I said before fish are cunning,
And lead many an angler a dance.

But seated by pond or by river
Away from the turmoil and strife.
I think that most anglers do it.
To be free for a while from the wife.

H Davis

Everyone

Everyone talks of the Yorkshire Dales
their beauty is outstanding.
All of us walk the hills and vales
where nature is abounding.
Everyone heed the weathered face
of the Yorkshireman expounding
and see the sheepdogs out at work
to help their master rounding.
Everyone goes to the summer fete
with the merriment and dancing.
And for ourselves a time to meet
and foster some romancing.
But when the summer's come and gone
and all the tourists too
we're left to think of other things
as well we often do.
Not everyone sees the winter time
when the blizzards can be frightening.
Or catches sight of the fallen tree
as it's struck to the ground by lightning.
Nor do they see the snowed in sheep
as the winter gales are heightening.
Nobody sees the toil and tears
that made this rugged county.
But everyone appreciates
the goodness of its bounty.

Trevor Berry

Magical York

Nowhere else, will ever be,
As magical as York for me.
Cameras click, and tourists stare
In wonder round the Shambles there.

Monk Bar, Bootham, Gillygate,
All relics of a bygone day.
Spring daffodils around the walls,
Proud regiment, in fine array.

Sunday boat trips sailing by,
Old Stonegate's shops, with treasures rare.
The Minster rising to the sky,
And choirboys fluting on the air.

The Maid of York, fair Katherine came,
From Hovingham's green wooded land.
She pledged her troth, and changed her name,
A royal ring upon her hand.

I wonder if the Knights of Old,
Go wandering still round Clifford's Tower?
And span The Foss in armour bold,
And laugh, and love, at trysting hour?

Oh, York is magical, and proud,
A jewel set in Yorkshire's crown.
Forever may its bells peal loud,
And bright stars light this little town.

Kathleen Rudd

Homeland

Morning mists caress the moorland -
Heather clad in purple hue -
Silent - as the night before it
Creeps the dawn - long overdue.

Farmers in their fields a-toiling
Sweet the smell of new mown hay.
Blossoms swaying in the breezes
Heralding the new-born day.

Sleepy villages awaken -
Cottages weave in and out -
Church bells ring across the valley,
Children sing and dance and shout.

Chimneys tall - Industrial County -
Noisy looms and clogging feet.
Shires nod and shake their tresses
As they trot down cobbled street.

Music from the bygone ages
Tears the very soul apart -
Greatness poured out from the pages
Stirs emotions from the heart.

This is Yorkshire - free and friendly,
Down to earth and worldly wise,
Yet - romantic in its splendour,
Seen with beauty in the eyes.

Yes - my homeland - land of loving -
Land my kinfolk left for me -
Deep, deep down my roots are planted -
Nowhere else I'd rather be.

Marie Hirst

The Sea

The sea is green, or blue, or brown.
It splashes up,
It ripples down.
The sea rises,
The sea falls.
The sea makes great big water walls.

The sea splashes and bashes and crashes.
The sea goes swirling,
The sea goes whirling,
The sea can whisper,
The sea can roar.
The tide can creep in over the shore.

Sarah Louise Wood (6)

Six Directions

We've six main roads from out of town, and no matter which we
                                                                         choose,
We need not travel very far to find some lovely views
First Bradford Road passed Hillhouse, to Fartown known of old,
For men who play at Rugby and wear the claret and gold.
We'll find the trees are sometimes just wearing the same shade,
As down the hill to Brighouse our pleasant drive is made.

Along Leeds Road and we shall see the other football ground,
And then we pass the ICI which world wide is renowned,
To Bradley too, we carry on, with Dalton on the ridge,
By playing fields and gardens before we reach Colnebridge.

The road we take to Halifax is the prettiest by far,
It has no trace of industry to leave an ugly scar.
For Edgerton itself is one long avenue of trees,
And the Bluebell woods round Grimescar have never failed to please.

Up Trinity Street and Westbourne Road until we join New Hey,
The lorries make their daily crawl towards the motorway,
But once we've moved through Marsh and Oakes and got to
                                                         Salendine Nook,
The hills each side of Outlane take on a bleaker look.

On the other road to Manchester the traffic's almost gone,
The mills down in the valley are closing one by one,
The cafes too are empty, their custom is so poor,
As no one seems to want to cross that vast expanse of moor.

But now we take the Wakefield Road and on it can be found
The slag heaps of the collieries, stood up above the ground.
They spoil the open countryside, but soon are left behind,
And then we see the TV mast, not ugly - not refined.

They think they've made a land mark, but it can't top Castle Hill,
It has stood there through the ages and we hope it always will,
On whichever road we may return, we can see its light above,
Just guiding us safe homeward to the Huddersfield we love.

M D Hollingworth

A Sheffield Evening

Late grey industrial afternoon
melting into a pink evening
over the Manpower Services building
at the bottom of the Moor.

That's when the starlings roost
on the shop facade ledges,
their shrill melody accompanied
by the hollow metal percussion
of market stalls being dismantled.

A man is playing lilts on a penny whistle
and wiping the spittle from his lips,
sat on the steps of Sheffield City Hall,
watching the passers-by and the mother
getting her baby to sleep in its pram.

And the soot-black immobile infantrymen
with their rifles and eyes downcast.
One with a rope wrapped round its throat
as if it had been hanged for some crime.

While the *Walking Man* wants to lecture
those winos that haunt the Peace Gardens
or get drunk down on London Road;
and a little feller called Charlie laughs.

When an old woman begs on the Wicker,
spreading her dirty hands out,
gathering small change for cups of tea
and crossing the road in blind haste
after every refusal.

John Critchley

Welcome

Welcome to Yorkshire
England's fairest county,
With open arms,
We share with you its bounty
Our rolling hills, our buildings old,
they welcome you,
Our joyful songs, our sunsets gold,
They welcome you,
But best of all is friendships hand
And this we gladly give,
In hope that you will come to love
This land in which we live,
To all our sights and all our sounds
Our buildings old and new
With joyful hearts and Yorkshire pride
We truly welcome you.

Madge Parker

Huddersfield Love

Friendly town of cloth and substance,
worthy town that grows on you,
chosen sample of the Northland,
by the comers-in, me too.

Solid town of work and commerce,
able site of industry,
and the home of choirs and music
that delights both you and me.

Proudly do your structures clothe you,
built honestly in stone,
showing a permanence to those,
who tread your piazza'd zone.

Where else is that Yorkshire mixture?
Churches, chapels of each creed,
Valleys, hillsides, town and country,
nurturing that unique breed.

The unique breed of Yorkshire folk
who take their cue from above
and like the good book asks of us
Call everybody *Love*.

G A Jones

My Yorkshire

As the years pass by and I look around at the Yorkshire
I knew as a little lad.
Of the friends passed by old and new, I find a tear in
my eye, and a chuckle in my voice too.
At all the antics we use to get up to.
The closeness and comradeship of the working class.
Amidst the factory's grime and dust.
The factories are no longer there, and the mines disappear
like the fading grass.
A hole has been opened by the Opencast
Like a Plague on the valley living in the past.
Artificial parks suddenly appear
Pizzas and MacDonalds spring up everywhere.
Is this what we really want for the young and old?
or could it be me that is getting old?
I think the Yorkshire comradeship still remains.
But at times, through lack of work becomes very strained.
But who am I to stand in the way of progress,
It's just my way of a little protest.

G W Scotrick

Penine View

I see from my window, gently sloping fields.
A silent road leading up to an old house,
The roof and chimney just visible,
With grey-black smoke curling upwards to the sky.

As I steal a glance from my labours at the sink,
Three or four horses come galloping down the field
As if their lives depended on it.

While in a nearby field cows quietly graze,
Sometimes I see one give birth in a quiet corner.
I see the red van in the distance,
And know the postmen will soon be at my door.

In summer on the distant hill,
Wild heather grows like a purple carpet,
Small figures like ants take the best of the bilberries.

In winter on the distant hill,
Snow drifts in from the moors
Revealing a world all white and still.

From my window I see the many seasons of change,
I'd love to paint each new pattern of flower and tree.
But I'm better with pen than brush.
I'm no Picasso - only me.

Betty Walton

My Yorkshire

Open doors and *cum in love*
Endless arc of sky above
Heathered slopes and weathered stone,
People shouting on the phone;
Ancient narkers -
Nosey Parkers -
All a part of Yorkshire.

Bronte moors, satanic mills;
Drystone walls dissecting hills
Shining windows doorsteps bright -
Cake and cheese on Christmas night -
Terraced houses,
Baggy trousers,
Comments tart in Yorkshire.

Choral voices raised in song
Karaoke sing-a-long
Woods and white cliffs, seaside sand
Coast to coast is almost spanned -
Friendly natter -
People matter
That's the heart of Yorkshire.

Hilda Kaye Gibson

Yorkshire

Yorkshire, greatest county of the north,
Acres of moorland, grouse, heather, gorse,
It has the dales, a sight not to miss,
God's picture painted, by angels kissed.

Cities, towns, villages, all worth seeing,
The people warm hearted, think of other beings,
Families deep rooted, all help one another,
Grandparents, parents, sisters and brother.

Folk in these parts are proud, loving, true.
Hard workers still, when the works there to do,
Times are changing, Yorkshire will live on,
Its arms out spread, reaching for the sun.

Muriel Rodgers

Its Name is Progress

Otley, my home town, where are you now?
The friendliness gone, it's all cold somehow.
Gone are the fields where our walks used to be.
Instead there are houses, with *aggro*, for free.

Our cinema's gone our dance halls, and all.
Instead there are pubs, with policemen on call.
I've longed for my home town, the place of my birth.
Instead it's the loneliest town on God's earth.

Gone are the days of the neighbour and friend,
When it was no shame to borrow, and so happy to lend.
Someone to chat to, a listening ear,
Now, they couldn't care less, that is progress, I fear.

Lyndis M Winterbottom

Betrayal

The soft swish of the shuttle, nevermore,
Will sail across the Northern textile sea;
For Yorkshire's soul lies warped against the door
Through which the sons of industry walked free.

No more I hear the clatter of the loom
Which thumped its demon music through my brain;
Now, silent voices speak across the room,
And silent sorrow falls like Pennine rain.

The moorland sheep cling sadly to their coats
'Ere proudly, once in nakedness, did stand,
But ash of millstone grit sticks in their throats,
As tears spill over houses built on sand.

Across the valley, blades of grieving grass
Take up their swords, 'ere Yorkshire's blood is spilled;
And men's souls cry and breathe with lungs of brass,
Resounding funeral bells o'er clouded hills.

What happened to the cloth of Northern gold
That Yorkshire hands embroidered in their blood?
Was our heart, too, for so much silver sold -
Betrayed by one, who in our garden stood?

Anne P Robbins

Snow on Yorkshire Moors

Silently: floating from
Leaden skies,
Drift myriads of white
Exquisitely shaped
Flakes. To settle,
And outline
In icy beauty
Moorland and tree.
A dazzling purity:
Harsh contours softened;
Cloaked; made gentle.
Beneath its soft mantle,
Earth sleeps.

Elizabeth Newell

Ginnie Lane

We've got a little Guinea pig
We've named her Ginnie Lane
She's got a pretty little face
You couldn't call her plain.

She's many colours in her coat
Like Joseph in the Bible
Her face one side is coloured black
With shades of white and sable.

She's only small, she's just a babe
They tell me that she'll grow
She sure can travel very fast
I wish she'd go more slow.

She makes a little squeaking noise
She really sounds quite charming
She charges fast around the room
It really is alarming.

We made for her a nice big cage
And put in lots of netting
We made a little darkened end,
So peaceful nights we're getting.

We've put her lots of sawdust in
And nice soft hay for bedding
A little dish with chopped up oats
A feast fit for a wedding.

Kathleen Pogson

My Yorkshire

The Dales of Yorkshire
stretch far and wide
with a thousand wonderful views.

The Tales of Yorkshire
are full of life the
stranger to bemuse.

The folk of Yorkshire
are kind and true
with a love deep and strong.

The beauty of Yorkshire
has been surely blessed by
the very hand of God.

Audrey Drake

Yorkshire

The beauty of the North York Moors,
The forestrys dark vale,
The heather's purple pattern cloak,
Scenes the senses do assail.

Homes of mellow Yorkshire stone
of dwellings so admired,
Tourists for this from far do roam
And are with enthusiasm fired.

The clifftops tower to the sea
they gird the rocky shore,
I revel this wild and windswept land
And will love it evermore.

Glenda Lawrence

I Had a View

I had a view, when I bought my house, of fields and woods and a
                                                                                                    river.
They've built a steelworks, on it now, and the view has gone forever.
I look out now, over rolling mills, a furnace shop with chimneys,
                                                                                                        smoking,
Belching into the atmosphere pollution from constant stoking.
Pylons straddle the grassy banks feeding power to the mills,
Looking like giants with outstretched arms dominating all the hills.

My other view, across the lane, was a field where barley grew.
They've built houses now, on that same field, crammed together two
                                                                                                        by two.
What once was open countryside now is urban sprawling,
Where neighbours do not say, hello, and no one comes a-calling.
The men, who plan and build these sites, go home to their country
                                                                                                         estates.
Their policy, not in my backyard, not outside, our front gates.

R Lewis

The Stare

Gazing at the flower's face
With a lover's attention,
I am suddenly aware
Of my gendered boldness.

She cannot turn shyly away.

No human creature would consent
To this scrutiny, nor would I dare
To reward such loveliness
With a stare.

John Earwaker

Hill Farm - Reluctant Sale - Divorce Pending

It's the twenty-fifth year and the twenty-fifth day
I am filing a life away
When to go and how to stay.

Flocks of lapwing ever growing
Bills paid and money owing
Curlews coming and swallows going.

Belching smoke and freezing draughts
Leaking roof and lots of laughs
Deep down inside some tears perhaps.

Bikes, horses and tennis games
With everybody changing names
Now and then low flying planes.

Blizzards, floods, inside and out
Someone giving the dogs a shout
Cats that won't ask to go out.

Meeting people down the lane
Whose cars will never be the same
Neighbours getting all the blame

It's the twenty-fifth year and the twenty-fifth day
I am filing a life away
I have a feeling of fear and pray

That when I leave I can be strong
And hope I won't forever long
To hear the skylark's morning song

Fay Blackburn

Unfertile Hopes

There are no flowers in my garden,
no butterflies or bees;
no green shoots of recovery
my aching heart to please.
No bright lights now shining
no sun filled rooms of cheer,
no great expectations
all hopes for the future
lay scattered by the breeze.
All that's left are memories,
and the prospect of the dole queue
to keep me now in line;
within this garden full of weeds.

K Casewell

Jewel of the North

Have you visited Doncaster town shrouded in a morning mist
Like a young girl waiting to be kissed,
Or seen the Old Market Place, spoke to the people
or captured on film their smiling face
If shopping is your speciality *Meridian Centre* is the place to be.
Many shops, for you to see restaurants and cafes and cinema's
If sport is your theme visit the Doncaster Football Team
The Dome will cater for your leisure or go to the races if this be your
                                                                                 pleasure.
Many Chapels and Churches for you to see
Many thriving sites of Industry
Railroad links from south to north.
Do trains run on time? Of course.
So forget about Spain and such. Doncaster is the place to be.
There are night clubs and pubs for you to enjoy.
Or have you tried a Bingo game, win or loose it is all good fun.
Parks to go for a quiet stroll, or a relaxing boat ride may be your
                                                                                   goal.
Many good newspapers, through which you could browse
The free press is very popular, full of detail in every way
Information to help you enjoy your day.
Come and see for yourself this lovely Town.
Doncaster won't let you down.

Lena Doherty

The Countryside

The tranquil and peace of the countryside
Is something to treasure, not something to hide
For a walk in the fields, the forest, the moors
Will bring peace to your heart for hours and hours.
To hear the sound of the leaves in the trees
Being quietly rustled, by the soft summer breeze.
When the lark from the meadow must surely fly
While bursting with song as it climbs in the sky.
The ripple of the water in the babbling brook
As it rolls over stones, then we venture to look.
The croak of the toad in the pond nearby
The splash of the trout as it catches the fly.
When the mist in the valleys, the dales and the dell
As the silence is broken by the distant church bell.
The colours you see, why no artist could paint
For they're constantly changing first bright and then faint.
The sight of the waving corn in the field
As the farmer prepares to harvest his yield.
The sounds that we hear, the beauty we see
Will always be there, for you and for me
And then the glow of the setting sun
Brings sleep and rest, as the day is done.

F Taylor

Crimsworth Dean Chapel

Turn off the Keighley Road, busy with tourist traffic.
Stroll down the twisting lane.
All around, a panorama of hills and fields
Stretches to infinity.
Here, at the end of the lane, is
Crimsworth Dean.
Built of Yorkshire stone, it is a symbol of
Yorkshire strength.
Stop, look, stay a while.
Peep through its windows,
Admire its simplicity,
Savour its strength,
Bask in the tranquillity of this rural scene.
Harebells, daisies and primroses
Flourish amongst the tough grass.
Its worshippers are few now,
But those few are the chapel's strength.
Time to walk on now,
But this spiritual gem remains.
A symbol of Yorkshire Methodism.

Fay Fielding

A Pennine Dawning

The morning air was bracing
As I stepped out of doors,
I stood and stared, whilst facing,
Those treeless miles of moors.

Brilliant shafts of light were racing,
Across the ancient view,
Until the sun came, gracing,
My world with sights anew.

I turned with thoughts engaging,
On chores still left to do.
The colours so amazing,
And the designs of nature, so true.
I dallied, wouldn't you?

Anne Penney

Green Gowns

Bare brown limbs, side by side they lie,
trembling and entwined, stark against the sky.
In naked ecstasy lost in nature's charm,
limb caressing limb, and arm on loving arm.

Sweet sap coursing swollen stems,
proud heads, fit for diadems,
bending and dancing to and fro to please,
unaware and unashamed, as they frolic in the breeze.

Fresh clothing, to adorn each single one,
radiant and shimmering in the golden sun.
Green gowns, how beautiful to see;
the trees have put their dresses on,
especially for me.

Brian Gregan

The Yorkshire Dales

One should visit the Yorkshire Dales
By walking, cycling car or rail.
Going up hills one meter in four
To see lovely views of hills and moor.

Wensleydale is famed for its cheese
Hawes, well known for lunches and teas.
Hubberholme, Keld and Dent have to be seen
With the hills and Dales covered in green.

Brimham Rocks, now a National Trust
So a visit there is certainly a must.
Also among some dry stone walls
There is a place called Aysgarth Falls.

Down to Pately Bridge and Dallow Gill
Then one goes up high to Gallow Hill.
There are many villages close together
And people tour around in any weather.

Mike Arrowsmith

The North

I live in the north, the north is the place to be,
People are generous, friendly and kind, you see.
Industry has gone, there are more on the dole,
It's a very grim picture, you see on the whole.

The north south divide is true I fear,
The south has the sun, the north has the beer,
They have the honey the sweet smell of money,
We have the grime the dole and the hard time,

Why does the south have the wealth and easy time?
Why should they get away with this crime?
The north would prosper if they gave us a chance,
This a blind man could see at a glance.

Working class man, whose backs the rich ride on,
Will work all day for a fair amount of pay,
But soon say nay to the capitalist way,
The way of more hours, more work less pay.

S Winder

Sheffield Parkway

Aluminium insects
cluster at the round,
crawling in a glistening swarm
towards the concrete mound.
One thousand heaving inwards
from carefully measured roads,
obedient to their schedules
and following the codes.

My engine slowly surges
then judders near a stall,
and the oily vapours hover
in the acrid pall.
The tall red light has stopped me,
but allows my stare to pass
around the ranks of faces
behind the rows of glass.

Let me note
that each face
is different -
as different as
I am.

The lights are turning green
and I push across the lines.
I'm surging round the island
towards the exit signs.
The others racing with me;
do they want the same -
to spin right out, and reach the space
which lets them have a name?

Mags Wigram

Yorkshire Pride

Come and visit Yorkshire,
You will have a nice surprise,
There is much to see in Yorkshire,
And the people are quite wise.

The scenic moors stretch out for miles,
The dales and hills, in splendour
Our stately homes, the gardens too
All lovingly attended.

Cloth caps and ferrets now are few,
But poets, artists, sportsmen renown,
You really must try our Yorkshire pud
With gravy thick and brown.

When the sun shines down on the cricket pitch,
With the players all in white,
A pleasant Yorkshire scene is this
On the long warm summer nights.

If you come to visit us
We will give a toast with beer
And when you leave our lovely shire
You will be full of Yorkshire cheer.

A Bellingham

Cold Doncaster

As the snow falls
Each flake is not the same,
All different from the last
That settles
On you,
The path,
The road.

Does it brighten your day
No!
You cannot see
The beauty of the day.

Do you look?
No!
You are too busy
With your hard face,
Looking for this or that
Bargain, to brighten your day
To bring a smile to your cold miserable faces.

B V Walker

Ode for the Ball and Chainers

One parent family's a wonderful life!
We're chocker up North, so they say;
With one in five families - we're bound to win through
And we're growin' in force day by day.
Now married ones worry, they oft put us down -
When we're 'appy as Larry, they think we're jus' clowns;
If we're grumpy or sad then they don't really ken,
They say it's because we're jus' desperate for men!
But we're not - for ther's nowt wrong wi' our lot up 'ere,
It's the ball an' chain families who's ever s' queer.
There's three extra wash loads a week in their tub;
They've gorra be 'ome to gi' 'usband 'is grub.
High 'lectric and Gas bills an' larders t' fill -
They can't go t' bed wi'out takin' a pill.
If yer talk to the 'usband, they think you're a huss-
When 'alf of 'em look like back end of a bus!
It's so sad bein' married - you argue the toss
'n the one wearin' trousers ain't forced to be boss.
For there's no 'appy families up 'ere in the North -
'cept for the ones which do end in divorce!
So get rid of yer 'usbands - 'n' 'usbands yer wives
'cos one parent family's a no hassle life.
You won't grey as quick an' yer temper won't flare
'cos it's only the partner you're with that's the mare.
Be in with *in* crowd - no trouble or strife.
Yes! one parent family's a fantastic life!

Marilyn Drozd

Words to Remedy Homesickness

The people all talk funny here,
Ee I don't know the things thi' say
When I go back to Yorkshire
They'll hear mi words and 'nay
You're not from Yorkshire that I'm sure
Bye heck you've changed, what shall we do?
You're *making tea* not
mashin' t' brew
Yer left these 'ere hills
An' went oft' to t' sea
What's Lowestoft got that we haven't got
There's no' but sea and sand
When yer get chance to be home you'll be here like a shot
Yorkshire's t' best, it's right grand
So wi' that we'll leave yer to yer fate
But remember Hebden Bridge is great.

Kathryn M Horner

High Pennines

I await the cornering of the bend,
Anticipation still strong after many encounters.
A wonderful feeling of time standing still.
The weather playing its part:
Sunshine is hope and peace and continuation;
Dark clouds and rain are a world we've lost.
It's just that particular vista, one main hill,
Where an ice-age has just ended, bringing new life,
Where I see my ancient men and wild beasts.
A scene hardly changed - for dreamers, like me.

E R Groves

Black Diamonds

Amongst the grime and coal dust
to the sound of rattling cage,
a weary group of miners
ascend from another cage.
All with eyes that sparkle,
teeth glistening, as pearls,
that shine from dirty faces
from their toil, below the world.

Each day the pallid faces
descend into the mine,
Fathers, sons, and uncles,
old, before their time.
Their days are spent like moles,
while we, the sunlight share,
they dig for the black diamonds
while we, breathe clean fresh air.

This proud dust covered army,
that keeps our land on top,
battle heat, water, roof-falls,
to keep our fires hot.
So in the north of England
that we all know as home,
there's a pride for our brave miners,
who provide our treasure, coal.

Hazel Collins

Yorkshire

Yorkshire to me is the place that I love
From the lowlands of Selby to the hills up above,
I've wandered the highways, I've walked on the plain,
But come back to Yorkshire, and I'll not complain.

We've Harrogate, Knaresborough, Richmond and Keld
There's Barnsley and Skipton where markets are held.
In springtime at Farndale, the daffodils blow.
Kirbymoorside and Helmsley, not forgetting Rieveaux.

The rhododendrons at Cawthorne are a sight to be seen
But Temple Newsman's display is fit for a Queen.
There's tulips at Round Hay, and crocus at Shelf,
The primroses at Wensley you must see for yourself.

In summer the roses bloom well in our Parks,
Greenhead, Beaumont, Norman, Ravensknowle before dark
We've Whitby and Scarborough, and Robin Hood's Bay
Filey, Hornsea and Brid for our children to play.

The Goathlands in Autumn are purple with heather
There's Ikley and Otley, let's hope it's nice weather
In winter, Holme Moss and Standedge you cannot get through
Snowdrifts on Tan Hill, Hawes Muker too.

The home of the Brontés is Haworth on the Hill
There's Hardcastle Craggs where we wonder at will,
Headingley for Cricket, Bradford for wool
Leeds, Wakefield and Ponte Cawood, Snaith and Goole.

Wainhouse and Shibden bring Halifax fame
Just think of fish, then Hull is the name.
Doncaster, butterscotch, Sheffield for Steel.
Colne Valley had textiles - Huddersfield - Robert Peel.

Coal mines at Emley and the Television Mast
Castle Hill is the place where they dig up the past
With Brighouse and Rastrick with band of renown
Heptonstall's unique Church, and York our County Town.

M Sunderland

England's North Land

These noble counties carved from ancient rock
support a way of life that's different from the rest.
We go on holiday to Norfolk, Wales or t' South
but always return to where we know is best!

We spend our summer days in peaceful bliss
on northern shores or on our scented moors.
Among our flowered fields and country lanes
roaming the land that's traditionally ours.

Romans, Normans, Vikings came and went
Let God's Own Country slip through their fingers.
They did not esteem its obvious worth.
Ravaged it, burnt it and left us the embers.

Years passed and we made it again to our liking.
Two World Wars later our lifestyle survives.
Visitors envy our unique surroundings
and continue to do so the rest of our lives.

K B Lambert

Cock O the North

If you lived in Yorkshire
This is what you'd get
Some fine upstanding people
And a welcome on the mat.

It's true we make good puds
It's true we race the dogs
It's true some men wear flat caps
Especially in our clubs.

Can you understand the Yorkshire lingo
Eeh bye gum and *let's gu tat Bingo*
Down at the Miner's Welfare Hall
To see if we can win it all.

So come up North
And try to be
A Yorkshire lass just like me.
Come to Doncaster
They call it *Donny*
Cock O' The North,
The girls so bonny!

Mary Fardell

Textiles

The textiles mills of today
Are the finest in every way
The years of skill and arts
Passed down by workers for a start.

Woollen and Worsted Cloth was made
In various colours, designs and shades
Skirts and jackets in check and plain
Costumes and suits in every style.

In plain or pin stripe too
Or new designs in grey or blue
It helped to keep us all in style
At home and world-wide.

Workers did their jobs with pride
Finished product was just fine
In Huddersfield we are proud to be
A part of the textile industry.

L Mansfield

My Old Man Keeps Pigeons

The old man's down allotments
He goes there every day.
His best friends are his pigeons
I wish *they'd fly away*
He gets up early morning
Has his breakfast then he's gone.
And he stays there 'til teatime
When hunger brings him home.

I am a pigeon Widow
To the old man - second best.
He's got a lovely big blue cock
That's sitting on a nest.
He talks about it every day
When he *lands* home for tea.
Then he has his happy hour,
And snoozes peacefully.

He sends his birds to races
To places near and far.
Poitiers - Le Mans and Rugby
And sometimes has *a jar*.
I think one day he'll triumph
If he can - beat the clock.
He's got faith - He'll win a race
With his big blue cock.

Mary P Linney

Dales

The old Dales farmer thinks a lot, but not a lot he says,
He's lived up here his whole life through, he's happy in his ways,
He doesn't need some office chap, to tell him how to farm,
Just keep away your pesticides, you will do his land harm.

Oh yes he drives a tractor now, and he makes his hay in bales
The old farm carts are ornaments, now sold in auction sales.
His home is full of good antiques, he'll not be taken in
With adverts, offering a good price, these things have life to him.

His Grandad bought the settle there, he's known it all his life,
The corner cupboards in the rooms, were brought here by his wife.
The old court cupboard, was a gift, from a farmer long since gone,
These things are *not* for sale! don't ask! they're for the farmer's son.

Some things have changed, you'll see a sign at the bottom of the
lane,
Advertising bed and breakfast, the reason is quite plain,
The old Dales farmer isn't daft, he knows a thing or two,
About letting out the best rooms, with the lovely valley view.

I really recommend this place, the view is far and wide,
The feather beds are comfy, and snug and warm inside,
The breakfasts are the tastiest, you've had in all your life,
How do I know the truth of this? Well I'm the farmer's wife.

Mary Hodgson

My City

Northern folk look at a derelict city,
Robbed of its greatness. More is the pity.
Huge booming hammers and furnaces bright
Woke up the people and lit up the night.
Cutlery workers and men who made steel,
Most of them gone now, it's all so unreal.
How could a city so prosperous and proud
End up like a bomb site awaiting a shroud?
Sports tracks and Arenas won't bring back the pride
Of the people who sorrow for the city that died.
Concerts and shopping, theatres and swimming,
Are only for leisure and not used for winning
The work that is needed to replace what has gone
From the city of steel. The place I call home.

B Elliott

A Northern Morn

As Boycott hits another magic hundred
The sweet smell of success
Intermingles with the orgy of odours,
Which dance like ghosts
Out of the stone wall kitchen
On that northern summer's morn.

16 Yorkshire puddings,
Sitting, waiting, smelling wonderful,
Very soon they will be leaving
Their little round abodes
Which they have been living in
Over the last hot twenty minutes.

A shout of *How's That?*
And then rapturous applause,
Suddenly woke the little terrier
As it lies in the kitchen corner,
Only to be confronted by
A large black pudding
Sitting alone on the side.

As the dirty pots become submerged
In the warm soapy water,
The sky outside turns grey and cloudy,
Match abandoned.
Rain stop play.

Aah, Yorkshire

Mark Hudson

The Statis Fun-Fair

Organs pipe loud in the damp evening air,
Sizzling fried onions with hot-dogs to share;
The *shrieking* of laughter as the Moon Rocket flies,
The Big Wheel keeps turning round into the skies;
Dogems go *sparking* along their steel base,
While Waltzers keep *spinning* as collectors give chase;
Air Rifles *crack* with three targets to win,
A white china dog or a lucky tie pin!
The Statis Fun-Fair with all its bright lights,
Its coconut shies and its fun loving frights;
But on with the season on autumn's fair coat,
With crimson gold leaves and sweet smelling wood smoke,
And watch rockets trace, high! Into the sky,
November the 5th with bonfires piled high,
Forgotten those moments of summer! and spring!
Let's laugh and be merry, let's dance and let's sing!

Barry Porter

A Scot in Yorkshire

The winding wolds weave patterns of brown
And green and gold against the wintry sky,
And to the east, a mist, like thistledown,
Enshrouds the clifftops where the seagulls cry.

What is the spell this county casts on me
Who always thought my homeland past compare?
Why do I feel uplifted, calm and free
Whenever I take time to stand and stare?

Perhaps 'tis that this beauty I now see
Is not an awesome sight wherein I feel
A tiny speck in all infinity
Or just a minute cog in life's great wheel.

For here is splendour I can understand,
Here, simplicity and grandeur meet
As if God is holding out his hand
And I am standing at his feet.

Nora Knox

Far off Church Bells

Watching whirling gulls
Battle into the wind
Off a crumbling cliff edge
This sedge-sown summer,
A distant drone involuntarily
Raises a hand against the sun.
From across the sea
The raider's wraith
Slowly reaches zenith.
Against a cornflower blue sky
Camouflaged grey underwings
Shine out white and
As the raider flies on
To pound Yorkshire's red brick,
Far off church bells
Mark time.

Stuart Alan Wroe

A Yorkshireman's Dream

Is
The racing page from the sporting life
A tender warm and loving wife
An allotment with a clear view
The cobblestones washed shiny new
A nice warm hearth and a mug of tea
An old clay pipe, and leave him be!
Bliss!
Bliss!
Bliss!

Helen Fardell

Yorkshire's Pride

Hear this the voice of Yorkshire's Pride
'Tis borne of stock so strong and true,
Of rolling hills and restless tide
Of winters white and summers blue.

In gladness do I wander by, the
Shepherds rise the fruitful plain,
A jewel to outshine the stars
This county is my pleasures' gain.

As blades of green the counties names
Emblazoned rolls of honour famed,
In past and present by God's own hand
Preaching of our joyous land.

With hardy heart and forthright tongue
Its folks would have you linger long,
To taste the pleasures that abound
From inland fell to coastal sound.

Though I tread the world's wide ways
In England's heart I'll end my days,
And when I leave this earthy life
I'll know the lie of God's domain.

Eric Langford

Yorkshire Life

Yorkshire is a sporting county
And the people there are quite unique
They learn a peculiar use of language
And have a strange accent when they speak.
The pits are all closing down
And steel is in decline
Soon there will be no jobs left
So folk may turn to crime.
Though the people there have little
They still find enough money to place a bet
But they always put it on three legged horses
Has anyone backed a winner yet?
Yorkshire is famous for its pudding
And the people certainly like their grub
They eat plenty of fish and chips
Especially on the way home from the pub.
The men go out dinner time and night
Because they like a drink and a smoke
They also play darts, dominoes and snooker
That's the life of the Yorkshire folk.

Joanne Jowitt

My County - My Home

The County of Yorkshire to me is home,
With the fells and dales people love to roam,
The Yorkshire moors with its contrasting weather,
misty mornings and wind swept heather.

The walled City of York we all greatly admire,
With the beloved Minster once ravaged by fire,
Museums, galleries, peacocks wandering free,
Cobbled streets to walk in search of afternoon tea.

Climb the steps to Whitby Abbey your cheeks all aglow,
See the fishing boats at anchor in the harbour far below.
Scarborough Castle in ruins stands yet it is still daunting,
The wind blowing in from the sea makes it chilling and quite haunting.

Sheffield the host of our Student Games,
The Disabled Olympics now one of its aims.
The Super Tram on which you soon may ride,
To show Sheffield City in all of its pride.

Historic chapel on the bridge, yes Rotherham is my town,
Kepple's Column, Clifton Park bring me joy when I am down.
Yes - Rotherham in bloom is a sight you should see
The streets in full flower all make this home for me.

Christine Johnson

Wordminer

Tribes of dammed exhume from a pit, worlds deep
Sculpted in coal, faith and face subsiding
in the sights of cold colonial cameras.
We dark savages somewhere to atheist everywhere.

Coal's drones rise to praise dawn's cool embers call.
Pilgrim's feet flow, stumbledown black hole, follow coaldusk dole.
Ebony opium seeps through cloister streets
and veins, an ancestral habitual hit.

Mammon's ministers glide limousined through
our dark shires to sack winding spires.
Stealing away hope before a lightless dawning.
Leaving a hole unfilled, surplus masses lifelorn.

Paganland's hearths flicker red wreaths
for our gasping son's silent sacrifice below.
My Grandfather, fossiled in a photo.
Face hewn by history, eyes worlds deep probing me.

Gone now, ashes to carbon, back to black . . .
The local God who moulded him,
and with these words I'll burn with him, perpetually.

Neil Fletcher

Northern Lands

Come to the north more rugged than the south you know,
But full of history is a delightful place to go,
Yorkshire County is exciting from Plain to Plain,
A foolproof beauty a place to visit again,
Doncaster is our noble town,
To me it really wears the crown,
York city the showpiece of the north here,
A place that you will return to year after year,
Historical, charming with a unique feel,
Country cottages, farms, meadows, you here
The church bells peel!
So much to show off to all around,
The northern showplace the happy-ground.
Each step you take in this glorious land,
Will fill your hearts with joy like a brass band.

Yorkshire's not only famous for its beer,
It's so intriguing a place of cheer.

Denise Frost

Pictures - in my Mind

I saw grey skies, with shadows of black chimneys,
I felt the wind go through me, wild and raw,
I knew the folks who toiled, in coal and soil,
Now heaven has claimed them,
For they are no more.
Gone are those days of chattering Towns,
With woollen mills and looms,
Housewives busy with children and their brooms.
Workers are still here, not in clogs, but boots,
Happy to return home to their own green grass roots,
Where skies are blue, with fresh clean air,
Buildings stand tall and high.
Now, the rolling hills and Dales,
Reach up to Northern Sky.

Val Wilkinson

Tramps

Drunks, down and outs kip here.
Stars are our only shelter, we
Use newspapers as blankets,
keeping out sharp winds.

A kiosk selling tea, coffee, grub
still not what we want.
A drop of the old dram.

Not a place when you're lonely,
hardly a beggar in sight.

Only an odd driver, and
curved line of buses for company
during our long night shivering at
the old pier head.

Malcolm Freedman

Thoughts on North York Moors

I could die here, forever winter.
Darkness, desolate and depressed.
A catalogue of entanglement,
Where happiness can never enter.

Life is a mystery, as granite tors,
Momentous, magnificent and magic.
Stark exhilaration of the soul.
I lay and bask on silent moors.

I can live now, in quiet peace.
Sunshine, sadness and solitude.
A haven for fraught minds.
Where expectations never cease.

A dream of hope, refreshed anew.
Light-hearted, laughter and love.
These feelings are part of me.
A confused mood because of you.

Josephine S White

Tadcaster Town

Tadcaster Town,
Is quite renowned
for beer and friendly faces.
The River Wharfe
has a winding course
and holds the local races.
The Romans came and named the roads,
we even had a battle,
Towton Moor lies two miles West
and now rears sheep and cattle.

Down the road is a City called York,
where American tourists visit and stalk.
The Yorvik Centre is full of fun,
not to be missed by anyone,
but should you prefer to hunt a ghost,
York have their own, or so they boast.

B Harrison

Motherland

The lady so stout, she watches him now;
This ravenous youth with his sprawling ideals
Off with his black dog mad at his heels,
Witnessing blows in this warring of worlds;
The roads of the yonder, their alien curls
Winding the hills like as strangling arms
Though here and there torn by the fracturing charms
Of the golden and green that glisten bare seen
By the youth's raging eyes.

He mocks the old lady, her wisdom and years,
As much to him now as his own childhood tears.
Believing in dreams, he dreams he is wild,
Wilder than hurricanes that hold him beguiled,
Wilder than snow and the flurries of storms
That wrestle the moors and bury the homes.
So, quiet and calm, she watches his play,
For she knows in her heart there's no more she can say.

She has watched as her splendour has shrunken and paled,
Drowned by a world that is stricken and failed,
A world that marauds over that which was free,
Makes ashes the wonders of all that could be.
But this ancient land loved of ale and of song,
With its men at the bails and its pride ever strong,
A people of stone yet of blood lightly won -
Though with memories of war and of justice ill done,
Never yield, with God's strength, never fly . . .

She knows the boy's heart has its roots in this soil
Though shadowed and harrowed by squanderous toils,
Emotions long buried now bellow and wail,
His spirit unleashed here can run on the trail.
This lady, so mighty, she watches him now,
Her love is unfailing, he feels it somehow,
Maybe near lost is his sense of his past
Yet she stands in the hope he remembers at last.

Neil White

The County Fair

The starting of a brand new day
The picnic's packed we're on our way
Now we've arrived we park the car
A country fair in a National Park.

Well groomed horses standing proud
All competing for a clear round
Clay pigeon shoots take to the air
Another attraction at the fair.

Marquees standing proud and tall
Judging taking place for one and all
Ice cream, popcorn, wine and cheese
Home made cakes and strawberry teas.

All the classes now have done
Competitors showing all they've won
People gradually drift away
Having had such a happy day.

We make our way back to the car
In this lovely setting of a Country Park
Homeward bound with all the traffic
The day we've had has been just magic.

D Bagshaw

Reflections

I think I must be like the weather,
But no! my thoughts I must now tether:
Inside the house, and inside me,
There's warmth and peace for all to see.

On the other side of my guardian pane
Are gales, black cloud and ho! the rain!
But I feel the love of those so dear,
In my full heart no room for fear.

And, gazing out upon the sea,
I know it can be calm like me;
Just now wind whipped with rolls of surf,
Tomorrow smooth as new laid turf.

These things to me are just new found,
There's so much beauty all around.
For in and out, I thank you Lord,
For granting me so deep accord.

Nan Bickford

North Country Birds

The cloud-bound tops hide raucous ravens,
But in the sun the golden plover calls,
While meadows pipits imitate the skylark
And wheatears flit and scold from whitening walls.

The lane has redstarts, wrens and robin,
The river shares the skimming swallows' flight
With wagtails three, and martins in the sand banks,
And rich reward of shy kingfisher's flight,

The busy dipper and the languid heron,
The scurrying red-legged water fowl.
As peaceful evening stills the busy farmstead
We thrill to eerie screech of hunting owl.

Margaret Lumb

Jam Jars of Delight

The days have gone - the times are past,
But still my childhood memories last,
And take me back again to when
My friends and I were nine or ten.

The smells of polish, chalk and ink
Invade my nostrils, when I think
Of wooden desks all shining bright,
Girls to the left - boys to the right.

In summer, jam-jars of delight
On windowsills for room would fight,
Bluebells, buttercups, campions too,
Cowslips, vetch and harebells blue.

On cold, dark days of winter snow
I still see, steaming in a row,
Bright woollen gloves - some large, some small
Along the pipes against the wall.

Our playground games are played no more -
Two-ball catch on the old green door,
So many chanting games we knew,
That we could play if wearing blue.

A glimpse of swinging washing lines,
Reminds me of those special times
When skipping dominated all,
And we stood breathless, by the wall.

To celebrate my fiftieth year,
Come birthday cards from far and near,
The senders still remember when
We all were friends - of nine or ten.

Cynthia Howe

Beloved View

Stand in springtime on a hilltop looking out across the Moor,
Where the hills are stained with purple and the grass a tender blur,
See the sheep, with lambs around them searching greedily for food,
Feel the pace of new beginnings and the stirring of the blood.

Sit in summer on that hilltop gazing out across the moor,
Cast your eyes on the rivulets snaking on the valley floor,
Linger on the black stone farms *Ash* Jackson loves to paint,
Which the country folk call *sturdy* and the Townies label *quaint.*

And autumn time is beautiful as seen atop the hill,
The russet, gold and evergreens defy the painter's skill,
And the gullies rushing water makes sweet music in your ear,
They'll become a frozen waterfall at the turning of the year.

The winter scene is different, a sombre sad affair,
With sullen skies and lowering clouds, and piercing cold the air,
The silence almost deafening and gaunt and bare the trees
The lonely curlews' calling carried softly on the breeze.

Stand any time atop that hill on the Moor we hold so dear,
Ask, 'Why do we hanker for *abroad* when we've got it all, right
                                                          here?'

B E Marsden

Septic Cut

Trapped between grassy towpaths
he lies sour and stagnant
drifting jetsam toward sluices
peeing between locks
pretending to be alive.

In his murky depths, puny pikes
hid in tubed bedsteads,
snap at minute minnows.
Tyres arched like giant eels
feed on a crust of a barge.

Beneath his undredged bed
spirits of wild Connamara men
lie with screaming banshees
cursing oaths at dead stout battles.

He swirls toward a sleepy wharf
where ghosts of bargees haunt deserted bunkers
cackle at rails rusting beside them
bemoan a sky line of smokeless stacks.

Tommy McLoughlin

Memories of Autumn

Steamed-up windows from a pan of boiling peas.
Innocent voices echo in a redbrick yard
In a gully walled of black slate.
Red runny noses sniffle and snort, in a sort, of rhythm.
Mother, watches over her flock from the doorstep
Hands on hips, shaking a beautiful blond head
Despairing the task of Monday wash.
As long soggy-socks steaming and darned
Are pulled from dollops of cold autumn mud
That somewhere hide Addidas and Puma
Their beaten soles treading the certainty of bald tyres.
Trousers with gaping knee-splits, plastered and stiff
By small-handed dexterity peeled adrift.
In a dripping iron grate the culprit rests.
A skin, wrinkled as an elephant's gut.
A bladder, smooth as a baby's butt.
The casey breathes gentle vapours in its peace.

Mother, still looking on with a belly growing by the day.
'How many flippin' more?' Is what I heard my grandad say.
A pan lid stutters its hot fury
As mother delivers her own.
Turns away to giggles and faces
As a mischievous raspberry is blown.
The yard rings to the joys of boys laughter
Smacks with the savour of beef stock and Yorkshires.
And like a gang of young gazelles
Four pairs of pin-thin legs leap the threshold.
And it's in for Sunday dinner.

Steve McDool

East Yorkshire Man's Dilemma

Never was I from Humberside
          from Humberside
Never was I from Humberside.
I took to me a Yorkshire bride
          a Yorkshire bride
I took to me a Yorkshire bride.
We lay and watched the Humber's tide
          the Humber's tide
We lay and watched the Humber's tide.
As a Yorkshire man I cried and cried
And politicians I deride
When they said me and my bride
Had to live our lives in Humberside.
Now all the tears I have dried
          I have dried
Now all the tears I have dried.
We are Yorkshire again me and my bride
          me and my bride
We are Yorkshire again me and my bride.
Living in peace near the *Humber's side.*

Ron Grantham

Scarborough Then and Now

What is this change?
Is it that they have bulldozed the Pavilion Hotel
Where a Laughton ruled, resembling his brother,
Henry the Eighth?
Lord Leighton's house is Woolworth's now, rectangular,
And such as he could not have dreamed to paint.
Is it just that old beauty, like a red rag
To a Council, has been killed
So all may look the same,
Like the young strangers in the streets?

Rowntrees smelled of luxury: had carpets every inch:
And the old cafe had fires, blazing
In tiled and iron alcoves;
Waitresses in black and frills: muffins in winter.

Why are streets crammed; ugly, jostling, seizing;
The small poor shops blazoned, with sales
Announced, misspelled, by splotch-posters?
Why do I run away, a fugitive,
Where once I came as lover?

Can half one century
Perform such battery?
On is it I, dimly remembering
Some illusory will-within
Towards order, peace, harmony?
All the same, then, it was there:
A something clear, pervasive
In the blue, sun-struck day,
That a war cleared away; some thing
Beyond all possibility of change,
Behind the visible air.

Derek Colville

A Miner's Lament

Don't go down the mine, my son, and have a life like me
Join the Army, see the world, and help to make us free
Don't go down the mine, my son, keep your feet firmly on solid
                                                         ground

Let someone else slowly die, in the bowels of the earth,
Where only black gold is found
Don't go down the mine, my son, the dust will choke your lungs,
And gradually fill your chest.
You deserve much better than this, you deserve the best.

Why did I try to persuade you, to reach out for the sky
I just didn't want you to suffer, and very slowly die
I tried to give you light, not passages filled with darkness and with
                                                              gas
Little did I know chemical and germ warfare would eventually
Come to pass
I tried to do what I thought was my best
Wishing you to succeed, a cut above the rest
I wish you had been a miner, my son
Not a posthumous hero, after the war was done.

Anne Dawes

Penned on the Pennines

As I gaze on Huddersfield
               and ruminate,
see the clacking woollen mills
               (which I hate),
grey canal and diesel trains
               gliding past;
chapels, churches, schools and shops
               radio mast;
hear the sound of merriment
               from the bars;
children laughing as they play,
               screech of cars,
all the warmth and happiness,
               all the fun
and the sound of cheering when
               a goal is won -

Though pleased I too can serve my town
               (alive or dead!)
I still prefer these moorland heights
               and heather bed.

But then, I'm just a silly sheep,
counting men, to get to sleep.

Marguerite C Guile

The Historic Town

The Historic Town where I was born,
It holds a royal status,
The river forth winds round like eight,
It is for sure a pleasing place,
The castle on the hill does stand,
It looks down on a Place that's grand,
It claims the right for what its got,
Yes Stirling Town has got the lot,
It holds for me sweet memories treasure,
And fills my heart with singing pleasure.

Anne Stocks

Crummockdale in June

The peppery scent of nettles
mingles with meadow-sweet. Blue geraniums
and yellow vetch, tall shining grasses
fringing the little path between stone walls.

Green sunny fields and clean white sheep,
closely-shorn, long thin necks and spindly legs.
On one side Pen-y-ghent, a stranded whale,
and Ingleborough's flat top on the other.

In the meadows, clover and bright buttercups.
We choose a pleasant field path
rather than climb to limestone Moughton Scar.
Clouds sail across the blue; the valley trees
are dark with summer; wheatears flash white tails,
flitting above the wall.

Joan Smith

Rain

Grey drizzling drops
Splatter from the sky,
Wetting concrete pavements -
Soaking as they lie
In murky deep set puddles
Trampled through by feet,
Muddied up by wellingtons
That protect legs from the sleet
That gathers as the rains pour down
In the streets of urban town.

Clear diamond drops
Sparkling from the sky,
Crystallising blades of grass -
Glittering as they lie
In puddles neath the hedgerows
Untouched by human feet,
Used as baths for hedgehogs
And making flowers sweet.
Rain is beautiful outside
Falling on our countryside.

Pat Mason

Four Seasons

Oh to be in Yorkshire when the summer rains softly fall.
To walk on a bright sunny morn and be greeted by the sweet
                                                          lark's call.
To feel the freshly cooling breeze and stroll through the swaying
                                                     fields of maize.
To sit and watch the sunset through the evening twighlight's haze.

Oh to be in Yorkshire when the autumn strips the barren land bare.
To walk on paths of fallen leaves and see my breath crystallise
                                                       the air.
To watch the squirrels gather nuts and prepare for slumbering days.
To wonder as scenes of colourful hues are replaced by those of
                                                   sepia and grey.

Oh to be in Yorkshire when the winter chill begins to bite.
To snuggle beneath the welcoming sheets on those cold icy
                                                   frozen nights.
To see my footsteps in the snow and flakes flutter from the sky.
To gaze at the frost upon the window pane as dark stormy
                                                 clouds go by.

Oh to be in Yorkshire when spring begins to show its carpet of
                                                      green.
To see the snowdrops begin to bloom and tulips paint their
                                                colourful scene.
For Mother nature to slowly stir and her beauty again to breath.
To see the miracle reborn again as each living thing conceives.

R A Fenwick

The Deserted Village

I passed by, one evening, at sundown,
When the shadows were slanting and long,
And there saw before me, in outline,
The shape of a village, long gone.
There were fields without walls, without fences,
Revealed in the daylight's last gleam -
Little platforms where once stood the dwellings -
A path leading down to the stream.
Here they lived, loved and died, in a village
Deserted long since, in the past.
The sun rose for them as it rises for us,
But neither for us will time last.
Here women once sat in the sunshine,
Talked and spun on a bright working day,
While their men folk were sowing or reaping -
Here, often small children would play.
What catastrophe forced their departure?
Abandoning home, till and hoe
To leave their familiar surroundings,
Was it plague, or crop failure, or foe?
Who were they, these shadowy figures,
Whose eyes viewed the hills I perceive?
Where did they bury their loved ones?
And who was the last one to leave?

You can still see the village in outline
And people it in your mind's eye -
But go when Earth gives up her secrets
As the sun sinks down low in the sky.

Margaret Throup Lancaster

Huddersfield my Town

A place to laugh
A place to cry
A place to call my own
Huddersfield - you mean to me
The world, yet you're my home.

A town of mills
A town of hills
A town of pride and promise
You have it all - heart and soul,
Strength, support and solace.

You'll forever be -
My home to me
My heart is always true
Huddersfield - my friendly town
I belong to you.

Jane Elizabeth Williams

Yorkshire Pride

Yorkshire is my county of which I am proud
I will sing its praises out loud.
Grey walled churches standing so proud
And within choirs are singing full of song
Feel peace of mind as you go along
Brass bands are marching playing to the throng.
We have bustling markets and vendors selling their wares
And people ride on moving stairs
Out of Town there are country lanes
You can walk and forget your pains
We have Abbeys and Cathedrals with large oak doors.
And castle on hills where battles were fought.
These were inherited they cannot be bought.
A beautiful Minster stands high in York.
With windows of coloured glass
And altars adorned with shining brass
These things you cherish as your days pass
Cricketers are bowling on lawns of neat green grass
While the Farmer works to bale his new mown hay
This is the place that I will always stay.
Our emblem is the pure white rose
Which is peace as God knows.

M Ward

Why?

There's a silence on the hillside,
There's a silence in the valley,
There's a silence on the streets where no one wants to tarry.
There's a silence in the shops where the tills no longer ring,
There's a wearisome in feet where steps have lost their spring.
There's a sadness in the voices as they collect their dole,
It's painted on the faces of the men who once mined coal.
There's no market for their product, or so they've all been told,
So they all became redundant, the young as well as the old.

'It happened to us too lads,' the steelworkers all say.
'We know what you are feeling; we too have passed that way.'

There's very little left of the town that we once knew.
Of the industries we had, there remains but a few.
Our town is sinking fast 'neath a blanket of depression;
The reason for all this, we're told, is simply a recession
But it's hard to watch a town, once thriving, slowly dying -
You'll forgive me, I know, if you should notice that I'm crying.

Margaret R Sayers

Ode to Almscliffe Crag

When quite a child, I looked at thee
With interest none.
For thou wert but a rock
Oh Almscliffe Crag.
Then as I grew, I made a note
That thou wert fair
More fair than many a place
Oh rugged crag.
Much older still I grew and watched thy moods
In seasons four.
And came to love thy many changing scenes
More than before.
In spring, thy rocks are touched with green
And buds awake
Around thy feet, as o'er the Wharfe thy gaze
Is steady, still.
In summer, people scramble up thy sides
And try their skill.
Then ramblers come and rest upon thy sward,
For there 'tis cool.
In autumn too they come, and feast their eyes
So much to see,
O'er hill and dale, pasture and harvest field
Golden and brown.
In winter, clothed in white and beautiful,
No traveller comes, 'tis quiet as the tomb
Then lucky we who live so near
See nature alone
And fill our eyes in slow content
With its perfection.

Gladys Mallinson

Fed Up

Why was I born a budgie?
Having to live in this awful cage.
With a feeling of frustration,
and inside an inner rage.
Some days I climb my ladder,
other days I ring my bell.
If only I could speak, the tales that I could tell.
Right now it's time for dinner,
a drop of water and some millet.
Why can't I have some salmon?
or a tasty piece of fillet.
Who's a pretty boy then? that's all I've ever heard.
Why couldn't I have been human? instead of being a bird.

T Broadbent

In a Northern Hospice

What silence among the flowers and birds.
You, still awake,
prone to a miracle that's lost its chance.
Can death be beautiful?
Or does it only smooth the guilt
of leaving you,
us, so alive?
But you would prefer
even dusty days to colours unfaded.
'Don't stay, it makes it harder to go.'
'Yes, my friend.'
How can the sun shine so
unshakenly?

Krystyna Lejk

In Harmony

Today the thought came to my mind,
while cycling.
'Would it not be good if people
could be as nice as their surroundings are.'
I looked at the trees, majestic in size.
I noticed the birds, singing away
and circling the sky in their joy
while feeding the young in their care.
Alongside the road
the hedges quite rough
with, in between, the blackberrybush
which, in due time, would give her fruit
abundantly and free
though picking is tough.
My eyes were directed to the sound
which my ears had caught from the field.
Horses were running, feeling loose,
nearby lambs jumping around.

The animals and birds and bushes,
it all seemed in harmony
and, as I pedalled alongside it all,
I thought for a moment
that feeling,
was also in me.

Countryside is like a breath of air,
pollution free.
Could only humans be like that,
in speech be pure and, in behaviour,
in harmony.

J Dejongh

The White Rose

A wild variation on an English theme.
A white rose stands defiantly amongst
the thorns whose roots creep lower,
Lodging tightly in the monochrome scene.

The silken folds speak through the black dust
which blankets in a warm, smothering fold
suffocating with each layer.
No storm comes to blow a gust.

Look, the stigma still remains there,
it breeds across the country
populating the fields of daffodils and poppies
rippled by currents in the air.

In its nodules is the key to life.
Someday soon a bee will arrive
and add a stripe of yellow.
Then again the glorious roses will be rife.

Penny Batchelor

Four Seasons

Your heart is the earth, turned in spring
Ploughed out, harrowed and rolled.
A seed-bedded
Sweetheart of gold.

Your heart is a meadow, mown in summer
Fragrantly forked up to dry.
A hay-stacked
Edifice of lies.

Your heart is a forest, mushroomed in autumn
Dog-sniffed and truffled with guile.
A cream-sauced
Recipe of bile.

Your heart is a mountain, frozen in winter
Untrammelled, uncharted and vain.
A piton-free
Pathway to pain.

David Clark

Sheffield - My Home

A Sheffield Thwytel bore he in his hose,
Was the famous connection that Chaucer chose.
A dirty picture in a golden frame
In some odd way, added to our fame.
For stainless steel was invented here,
And Sheffield Plate, the Victorians held dear.
Posh ladies declared with accents funny,
'Yes, my dears, where there's muck, there's munny.'
The recession came in and trade grew less,
New thinking must get us out of the mess.
Scientists worked hard and very soon,
Our instruments helped in landings on the moon.
Sheffield's fame in science galloped on apace,
When Helen Sharman rocketed into space.
Joe Cocker and Def Leppard are famous in *rock*
And *Wednesday's* name is one you can't mock.
Michael Palin schooled here, before travelling was led,
Mary of Scots *prisoned* and then lost her head.
The golden frame is still there for you and for me,
With moors as far as the eye can see.
Quaint little villages, made out of stone,
With the odd Stately Home to add to the tone.
Chatsworth is near, Haddon Hall as well,
Eyam's not far, with the famous *Plague* well.
Our streets are riddled with craters like the moon,
But Supertram will be coming to all very soon.
Oh we may be down, but certainly not out,
When we've so much going to shout about.

Vera Percy

A Visit to the Summer Exhibition

Do ring 'er Miss Stringer
we have to know
what time to meet.
She said we would be meeting
by the Odeon, Main Street.

Be sure to take dear
your own packed lunch she said.

Course we've only one stop there
and little time to get fed.
We,
don't stay all day dear
the walking gets too much
and seeing as
it's just once a year
Madge and I taxi off to Harrods.
Have a cream tea treat,
go Dutch.
Though it's entirely up to you
what you do do
once you're there
just make sure
you're back at the coach
by five thirty
Trafalgar Square.

Geraldine Outhwaite

Twixt Lancashire and Yorkshire

With dry stone walls
And sheep that graze
The fields stretch out like one large maze
While way beyond the Pennine way
Yachts sail out on a clear blue day
A motorway network cuts straight through
While streams wind down
To take their cue
One patch of nature left unspoiled.
For folks with dreams or minds to uncoil
A picnic area for children to play
While parents watch on a sunny day
Or if one likes to take a stroll
A quaint old Church to cleanse their soul.

Mary Chadwick

The Visionary

The visionary sits alone in a dream
Creating a mystical and haunting scene.
Voices tell him where he must go
How to get there and what he must do.
He raises his body and walks in a trance
He's giving the world its final chance.
A path opens up and lets him through
What next? . . . Where to?
His lips move but no sound is released
He's chanting silently, calling the deceased
Rising them up from the bowels of the earth
Breathing new life, giving rebirth.
The emergence of life through resurrection
Pushing the world in a new direction
A flame of hope slowly burns
As the visionary stops and turns.
His face is hit by the flickering light
Softly he smiles, then fades from sight.

Claire Collins

My Home Town

Huddersfield is a really splendid town
With Choral Society of world renown
Many choirs also male voice, ladies and voices mixed
All very keen with their eye on conductor fixed,
Our musical traditions in all fields are strong
All working hard to give us a tune and a song.

Water from surrounding hills the River Colne do tame
Making industry able to give our town fame,
With Boilers, Tractors, Valves and Woollen Worsted too
The industrial revolution we did pass through,
When cloggs, cloth cap and shawl went with the job
Works hooter sounding meant they could earn a bob.

A man we had who Prime Minister became
Harold Wilson was his name
The roots of James Mason in Marsh can be found
A film star of great renown,
Ibbotson and Lonsbrough came from here too
To mark your achievement we named flats after you.

Fine stone buildings surround our station square
A façade of which it's grandeur is rare,
With castle sitting on distant hill
And Scammonden Dam which rain do fill
With countless mills which Lowry on canvas shows
And stone houses standing all in rows.

The world is an oyster of sights to see
Travel brochures display their details for people like me,
But journey over and homeward we roam
From where Moonrakers and Golcar Lilys were unknown,
To streets where Examiner is daily on sale
This is the Town from which I hail.

M M Walker

Lakeland

Clouds came down on the hills today

Summits were lowered,
Tree lines lopped,
When clouds came down on the hills today.

Jagged crags were softened and smoothed,
Falls of water lost in the mist,
When clouds came down on the hills today.

Walls of stone and woollen sheep
And birds on the wing faded away
When clouds came down on the hills today.

Clouds are clear of the hills today

Summits have peaks,
Tree lines are sharp
While clouds are clear of the hills today.

Jagged crags pierce the sky
And falls of water waltz in the sun
While clouds are clear of the hills today.

Walls of stone and woollen sheep
And birds on the wing in the wind
Are plainly seen in the freshening air

Clouds are clear of the hills today.

John Potter

Scunthorpe v Rotherham

Doncaster. I can hear the edge in my voice
Telling the children
To hurry this is our stop.
Aren't you going to let them say goodbye
To him he kept them occupied,
His mate catcalls after me,
Who's bumping down the gangway,
Makes my cheeks red, my eyes blink furiously.

We've had a lovely day out.
Going home the train is full of fans,
Jubilant they must have won.
I'm glad.
It makes the journey more reassuring.
Except for you a couple of rejoicing pints too many.
My children enjoy your funny faces.
Not understanding the menacing undercurrents
That undermine my matriarchy.
I am losing control, overreacting,
Reduced almost to tears.
The man in the suit colludes with you,
Turns to tut-tut as appley fingers
Stick him up.

I'm watching you (you didn't know that),
Although never looking directly
But reflected in the evening blackness window.
You are too merry to see my bristling self-defence.
I am embarrassed and ashamed aren't you.
But most of all I hate you.
I won't excuse you're lack of forethought
You're bit of fun,
At some other woman's expense.
Just because you're drunk.

Am I making too much of a silly isolated incident
On a train. Probably.
But I said in my more confident moments,
I wouldn't be walked on, stepped on, stamped on,
Gleefully anymore by any man.
But it's the vicious circleness of it all
That makes me too weary to complain.

Lesley Marshall

The Fallen Empire

Once a thriving empire stood and raised it's pennants to the stars,
And danced its reels on spinning wheels midst webs of pipes,
                                        and iron spars,
In spite of that, and wealth begat, the Empire's flat:
                            Its space the landscape mars.
The silvered rails where Wagons ran; the Gantries, and the
                                      aerial road
That *flew* each skip from mine to tip as endlessly they to'd and fro'ed;
the cooling towers that *steamed* for hours and shed their *tears*
In mist like showers and distilled waters sowed;
The joiners shop, the blacksmiths too, that *sang* to whine of
                                        saw and drill;
The sparks that fled from anvil's bed, and grindstones turning
                                        loud and shrill;
All gone alas, part of the mass which later years turns to grass:
                                      the sugar on the pill.
The boiler house: The colliery's heart from which its power of life
                                        once sprang,
Provided power for bath house shower that cleansed the
                                  pores of the coal blacked *gang*,
And wound the *thread*, from base to bed, on drums on
                                      headstocks overhead
Where winding wheels once *sang*.
The offices of pay, and weigh; The cabin where the lamps were
                                            trimmed;
And high imperial (managerial) the office where the cream was
                                            skimmed;
All turned to blight, snuffed, like a light; vanished from the
                                        pithead site.
Its sight forever dimmed.
Where Askern's small coal empire stood, and bravely waved its
                                          flag of state,
Now Old King Coal, with begging bowl, stands waiting by the
                                          pit yard gate;
Despite entreaties by the horde that it's wealth could be restored;
The pen proved mightier than the sword and *wiped* it off the slate.

A mining town without a mine: A life without a future's thread;
A sorry sight by day or night, an Empire that's expired and dead:
Ghosts now roam the mine shafts well, and wander through
                                                    its empty shell;
Silently the scream and yell for comrades fled.
How many more coal empires fall before the world is satisfied?
Yet the price of coal pays not the toll for all the miners who
                                                               have died.
Even they who paved the way for fortunes made up to today
Have little left to *give away*, except perhaps their pride!

Ben Stone

Cleethorpes

Upon a *bright?* and *sunny?* day,
Up to Cleethorpes we made our way,
For my Grandma's sake we went
(Back home I'd rather be sent!).

There was litter, litter everywhere
Not in bins; just anywhere,
Ice cream and hot dog vans all around,
Not a square yard of spare ground.
There were toffees, lollies, ice creams galore,
Most of which were stuck to the floor!

People standing, sitting, laying,
I can't understand why they're staying.
People wandering slowly about,
But move fast when the odd kid shouts;
Lots of dogs, roaming free
Sending children to their parents' knee.

The smell, the smell was really ghastly,
It made you think of things quite nasty;
Mustard, hot dogs plus the odd *chip*
Mingled with pollution from the passing ships.
Not here the white clean sands,
Nor the green distant lands,

But pollution all around,
Spreading litter on the ground.
Not the calm unpolluted sea,
(You even had to pay a car park fee)
But a sea, polluted far
By horrid things such as tar.

No sea birds (they've got more sense)
Than to see a sea which is so dense
By, like I say, pollution and more,
By people listening to the sea roar,
So heed this warning and don't go there,
It's much better to go elsewhere.

Jane Marriott (12)

The Scarborough School

Here we are were on the train
Going to the school again
there to meet friends old and new
Listening to the things they do.

We arrived all safe and sound
Had dinner at a place we have found
Then on to the hotel we go
To find our rooms and start you know.

Into the lounge we all must go
Listen to the chat go to and fro
Old friends new friends all to meet
Getting all the news is so sweet.

Discussion time is here again
So groups are planned that's quite plain
Suggestions fly to and fro
The right we think is plain you know.

Now its time to have some fun
For the work has now been done
The hat parade was such fun
Such a joy for everyone.

Then the pianist loud and clear
Played the tunes that bought such cheer
Everyone joined in the songs
Spreading love to everyone.

So that now we are homeward bound
Farewells are called to all around
See you next year was the cry
As we turned and waved goodbye.

Mavis Hall

Waterbaby

It appears with the suddenness of a giggle,
bursting from beneath a clovered coverlet,
its birth a black mystery
hidden deep in the hillwomb's history.

there are no mercatored projections
to this dimple on the face of the hill,
only a terse set of directions.
north of Broadstones Res
and south of Four Lane Ends,
west of Birds Edge
where the windbent beeches
are a line of Muslims at prayer.

disappears into a narrow defile
in the arms of earth mother, gurgling
its song under a plovered sky.
begins to wire up the valleys
taking tribute and tributaries,
a pennine emissary
to the blackarsed denizens
of Darton and Barnsley,
Bolton and Wath.

Christine Ross

Yorkshiremen are Barmy

Yorkshiremen are barmy, I know 'cos I'm one mesen.
There's sommat about being Yorkshire
That sets thee apart from ordinary men.

Now a Yorkshire lad's got five interests -
And these I'll set down in my text
They are ale and racing - cricket, football and sex.

Na then, take ale, (as a Yorkshire lad frequently does)
The ale down London is shocking - it just in't worth a shout,
Down thee're when they say, 'It looks like rain.'
It's the beer they're talking about! - It really is that bad -
But up 'ere it's champion and as strong as a Yorkshire lad.

And when it comes to racing and looking in t' 'orses mouth
We keep all t' winners up 'ere and send all t' losers down south.

Cricketing times are different now but I can remember when
Any Tom, Dick or 'Arry could play for Kent but if thy wanted to play for Yorkshire
Thy 'ad to be Yorkshire thissen.

And when it comes down to football no-one can say ther's owt up -
But we keep upsetting t' Southerners by going to Wembley an' winnin t' cup.

And when it comes to women, t' Southerners might 'ave all t' brass
But any Yorkshire lad knows there's nowt like a Yorkshire lass.

So you see we live in Yorkshire 'cos Yorkshire's got all that's best.
So we'll stick wi t' biggest county and t' others can 'ave all t' rest.

Now we might lack *sophistication* (that Southern guile and craft!)
And we know Yorkshiremen are barmy, but, by gum, we're not that daft.

Steve Sheppard

The North

The beautiful north,
I love so much,
My home town in the north.
My fondest thoughts and
treasured memories,
lies deep down in my
heart for the north.
If I could, I would relive
my childhood days spent here
in the good refreshing north.

Lorna Montaque

The Last Bus Stop

It was siling down at the University
bus stop. Would the last one ignore us
for spite, as usual? 'Bleeding students
let 'em walk . . . do 'em good . . . hope they drown.'

A famous poet; tall, bald, bespectacled,
sloshed up behind us. His asymmetrical
features, stoop and sober tie were a match
for the weather. He was obviously drunk!

Suffering from an overdose of words -
a skinful of poetry. A black brolly
kept him one-hundred-per-cent waterproof,
but that formidable talent was off on

a permanent sabbatical and was muttering
to itself about something *going off the boil.*
How does it go, that old Yorkshire saying:
from Hell, Hull and librarians, et cetera.

We closed ranks against the living-dead.
'Don't think you're coming under my umbrella.'
That place will never be the same again:
come to think of it, it never was.

Pete Haythorne

Doncaster

When Romans came 55 BC
And built the Great North Road,
They established it as a trading place
Whilst Brits were still in woad.

The Anglos and the Saxons came, then
The Pagans sacked the town.
When the Normans conquered Doncaster,
Again, it was burnt down.

It boasts that Richard Lion Heart gave
It a Royal Charter.
The trading folk continue, here, to
Meet and buy and barter.

Invaders now are welcome and with
Friends they're sure to meet.
Visit Doncaster market and have
History 'neath your feet.

M E Lavin

Conisbrough Castle

There is a river flowing by
A hill with castle and moat
Although for kings of long ago
It may not now be so.
A monumental effigy
Towering above the road
Reminding us of what once was
In a life long, long ago.

Deer would roam the Conisbrough Parks
By a hill with castle and moat
Although for kings and not for all
We read in *Ivanhoe*.
A view for miles around
From the stoney walls
Reminding us of what once was
In a life long, long ago.

Sunset closes high on a hill
Throwing shadows over the moat,
It may not be the *keep* it was
But guards us to and fro.
From Warrenne to Plantagenet,
King John and Richard too,
Reminding us of who it was
In a life long, long ago.

Gwen Bedford

The voice of Micklefield

I like to hear the village churchbells
sounding long and loud and clear
Like a sweet song from Heaven
Telling me that God is near.

I love to hear the cuckoo
Heralding the sound of spring
And the dawn chorus of the sparrows
How I like to hear them sing.

I listen to the sounds of the Countryside
they make my glad heart rejoice
The dear old countryside of Mickelfield
I harken to its sweet voice.

The churchbells of St Mary's
the cuckoo in the Hartley Wood
The sparrows in my little garden
Are a tonic to do me good.

The brass band is hard at practice
So is the male voice choir
Echoing all the village goodness
What else could listening ears require.

I love to hear all the various sounds
That make the voice of Mickelfield
They create a unique song of Heaven
And my joy cannot be concealed.

Dennis Best

Yorkshire Images

Let me take you for a ride around the glorious Yorkshire Dales,
See the rivers and the rippling steams that run from hill to vale,
Let me show you Semerwater with its tiny river Bain.
I feel very sure you're bound to want to visit it again.

There's Fountain's Abbey, Studley Royal, Bolton Abbey and the rest
You will agree, I must insist, they are all the very best.
Drive along the road to Bridlington, Scarborough and Grimsby too
Try the *pot holes* and the caves, but be careful what you do.

The Humber bridge that spans the river which leads you to the coast
Is absolutely beautiful and I'm not one to boast.
Take a fishing trip to Grimsby, and at Whitby see the jet.
Come walk with me along rambling moors, that are the finest yet.

To end our journey I must not miss York Minster's glorious sight
It stands out clear and beautiful in floodlight or moonlight,
May its choirs sing on forever, may they always give delight,
May the sun shine down forever, may its image be always bright.

Vera Hansson

All Rounder

If I could bat as well as I wished I could.
With an array of strokes to improve the score
Striking every ball sweetly off the wood
Like Holmes and Sutciffe in times before.

If I was fitter and maybe a little quicker
Like Trueman leading some county's rout
bowling bouncers and yorkers. The odd in swinger
to make those batsmen leap about.

If I was artful and had the skill
to deploy some cunning strategy.
I'd baffle with subtleties of spin
then bowl 'em out like Verity.

In the field my handling safe and slick
prepared to hurl myself around.
To throw or catch like Sharpe at slip.
Anything to keep the total down.

Once I'd honed these unknown talents
and in a team whose strengths were unsurpassed.
A team with style and flair and balance
then Lancashire would really be outclassed.

Keith Jenkinson

Three Haiku From the Dales

Gilded buttercups
flow to the river's bank
rusted with sorrel.

Ice roses Wharfe spun
fashioned from frozen flood foam
floated by the bridge.

Roots deep between stones
wallflowers frill high battlements
loud haunt of jackdaws.

Marion Sinton

Second Childhood

Midsummer and a madness - child again -
A class of *Twenties* children - *nature walk* -
We hear our Teacher's voice: she now and then,
A shepherd of her sheep, says, 'Walk, not talk!'

We go up old Cow Lane, agog with glee -
They call it School Road now - a heaven no more -
Inside ourselves we skip for we are free:
School lies behind us and the world before.

We are at home in this our heritage.

We grind the gravel grit beneath our feet
As two by two in harmony we plough
Our way past hedges green and sweet -
That *bread and cheese* is hawthorn, we know now.

'Walk on and climb the stiles!' our Teacher calls.
Above, blue sky, a yellow sun; all round,
Green fields, green trees, now buried under walls
On walls that vainly hope to hide the murdered ground.

What have we done to our child's heritage?

And next come five white ducks for our delight
Up ending on their duckpond in the lea;
And last my field of corn, a golden sight
With bright red poppies growing just for me . . .

My cornfield and my poppies - where are they? -
See, foolish child, arrest your wayward fears.
You have kept them in your heart until this day -
Ah yes, I have found them here among my tears.

A pity, they will say. It is her age.

Doris Wilkinson

The Pigeon Fancier

If Billy's pigeons do it once more,
And I see them from my back door,
I'll run down my path,
Folks'll think I've gone daft,
And at the top of my voice, I'll scream.

Keep them bloody pigeons you've got, on your side,
Or I'll tell the council, that you flaming well lied.
About how many you keep in that shed,
And how their lodger, the rat, is really well fed.

        Them Pigeons.

Those mucky sods, do it all down my sheets,
It's nothing new, it's been happening for weeks.
I'm sick of their droppings all around,
In fact when I look, It's all around.

So keep them on your side, Billy my lad,
Or you'll be the one who's sorry and sad.
For in the near future, I'll purchase a cat,
Then send him over to play;
With your pigeons and rat.

Elisabeth Barlow

Sonnet to Lakeland's Autumn Loveliness

Through summer's passed and birds are on the wing
To warmer climates: Though daylight earlier dies,
And sap to earth descends; no room for sighs!
The trees in autumn loveliness now bring
Their maker rightful praise: and mellowing
To richest hues of reds and browns, we rise
To ecstasy, as smiling sun supplies
Its own kaleidoscopic colouring:
Observe from trees in gold by season cast,
How unassuming gratefulness is sweet;
When shorn of beauty by unbidden blast,
They humbly lay their glory at our feet:
When winter rudely storms our creaking door,
Shall we be gold to pave that heavenly floor?

Christopher R Shaw

Up Beyond Moor Lane

Walk along Moor Lane late at night
To the fork and beyond the last road light.
Walk along to where the ground is raw
And the lane winds up to the higher moor.
Climb hard up the track as high as you can
To where night's darkness envelopes the standing man.

Here the cloud scudded moon silhouettes the distant farm
And glints on the roof of the rain soaked farm.
Feel the wind sting your ears like the words of that bitch.
Listen to the rain flooding by in the trackside ditch.
Look down on the monoxide town below
As still higher up on the moor track you go.

Now here on the top of this rain sodden land,
Windswept and bleak where this sullen man can stand.
Away from domestic passions, factories and fumes;
Away from picture boxes and numbered rooms.
Here, a top this passionless moor an ordinary man, alone can be
And breathe the sweat perfume of common sanctuary.

From cot to coffin, sperm to ash,
As through this life cycle we make our dash,
Take time to ponder, up beyond Moor Lane
And sense the pulse of natural life again.

Martin Dutton

Our Lovely Yorkshire Moor

How strong - how brown - how dirty looks like heather
On our lovely Yorkshire moor.
The bogs are deep with rain and melting snow,
But soon all will be purple, like a soft veil of silk
And the white of the sheep, and the black of the dogs
Shine through, as a beautiful patchwork quilt.
The breeze will be gentle, and the cotton flowers away in the sun.
The lark will sing in the heavens, and the mother grouse forage
                                                    for her young.
The bees will gather pollen, and the butterflies flirt and play.
And the shepherd will gaze with pride at his sheep,
On our lovely Yorkshire moor, one day.

Hannah McAndrew

Yorkshire Born

If you were born within her bounds
Your first breath drawn of her
If your first faltering steps embraced her soil
Your childhood spent
Exploring her myriad acres
The same in number as the Bible's words
If you grew in Yorkshire - anywhere
In her moorlands, dales, or industrial heart
How favoured you are to be part of her
Part of her Heritage, history and the splendour
No other displays, such panorama as this
From the Pennine tops to her cliffs and bays
Which shape her coastline, edging her sandy shores
Where the summer children play
But should you leave her for distant lands
for peaceful journeying or the demands of war
Pretend not, that you leave with ease
Shaking off the gentle hold she has on you
She will let you go, but keeps you shackled still
With invisible chains binding you to her
She never, never will let you go, completely
For in quiet moments your thoughts will turn
To all you knew of her, and in your heart
Memory will rankle
Pulling as a magnet pulls, until resistance falters
You make your way back to her
Not ever understanding - why?

Dorothy Mason

Ingleborough Contrast

Cave cold we followed our guide
Wary of the slimy slabs of rock
Plopping sounds punctuating the explanations
As our attention was directed to
Cascades of blue translucent ice
Or stalagmite and stalactites
Formations, transcending modern art,
Entering low narrow passages
The groups postures ape cavemen
Until, straightening again, each is silent
Introspective, touched by times beginnings

Emerging, the sun wraps with invigorating warmth.
Released, aching, chilly backs
As eyes adjust to brilliance of grass.
This bouncy steam bears no relationship
To that reptilian flow snaking the cave
The multi stickered van attracts
Ice cream, ice age
Bridged
By a flavour.

I Taylor

Returning to Flamborough Head

We found the caravan site as we had left it:
Old worn footpaths took us to living memories.
Arriving at the same time of year,
We watched the combine harvesters
Patrolling the fields, ever nearer the cliffs.
Thornwick and Sea Farm were grafted together,
An organic flock of intimate lives
Honeycombed onto the hill
And hedged in from the sea.

Walking down the lifeboat run was like
Diving over a cliff. When we reached the bottom
We found the caves cut off by the tide:
I think we'd expected to find
Fossils of our childhood in them.
The walk along the cliff tops from
North landing to South landing was
Our personal pilgrimage to our favourite deity:
The lighthouse. We had seen its beam from Scarborough.

Reaching it, I looked back towards
Thornwick Bay and watched the sun
Glazing the roofs of the caravans.
Every night, and every morning, was
Crammed with smells, tastes and colours,
Like a sweet jar. They returned to me
Now, actual sensations, not memories.

Today I caught up with
The part of myself I'd left behind
Ghosting around the caravans,
Throwing wheat darts,
Laughing.

Jim Hart

Poetry of the North

Life in the North of England
is better than in the South
there's more to see and more to do
and everyone will be nice to you

Whether your from far off Pakistan
or from across the Irish sea,
You'll find a welcome in our faces
As we point you to the nicest places.

There's Ilkley Moor without a hat.
It's rocky, barren, cold and windy.
Where someone's been courting Mary Jane,
Even though I've heard she was quite plain.

Halifax has now been made quite grand.
Since Prince Charles paid a visit.
Though the Gibbet's still on Gibbet Street
Where our friends from Pakistan love to meet.

Bradford is now a holiday spot
Why or when I'm not quite sure
If you like crowded streets and buildings tall,
You might not mind the smog at all.

There's Otley, or is it Beckindale,
Or maybe, it could be Emmerdale.
There's hen's and sheep and cows to see
And Annie will make you a cup of tea.

So come to the North and see for yourself,
Our ups and downs and hills and dales,
When on these hills you start to roam.
You'll never want to go back home.
Honestly!

P Watson

Yorkshire Talk

Up here in 't North, if you're down in the mouth
Tha should pack up thi bags and go and live South
We're a very happy breed, I don't really know why
But if you go around moping, now and then give a sigh
Pull a long face, not showing much glee
Somebody will shout 'What the hell's up with thee?'
We have our ups and downs and our ins and outs
Some of us are quiet but some of us shouts
We're the salt of the earth, of that there's no doubt
If tha doesn't believe it I'll give thee a clout
Gravedigger Ted, in Yorkshire, when asked about his work
Said 'When somebody dees, there's no time to shirk
I measure out the grave, two and half feet by eight
Then dig down deep and mek the walls nice and straight
Then on 't day o' t' funeral, with artificial grass
I spread it around t' hole and mek it first class.
'It'll be neat when it's finished,' the questioner said.
'Nay, I'm finished by dinnertime,' said gravedigger Ted.
We're all comics in 't North, we've no time to frown
Tha mun smile at everything and act like a clown
They come up from the South, they think we are thick
But they'll have to rise early, to teach us a trick
Lots of us are colliers, and this is no joke
We've often had a shift off, when our dudley rope broke
You can rely on us all and this is my oath
We'll never let thee down, 'cos we're folk from up North
We're God fearing people, we stick together like glue
Not much upsets us and we speak straight and true
We work hard and play hard and enjoy our beer
And I'm really convinced that God came from here.

Jim Armstrong

Springtime

The birds are singing lambs are bleating
Flowers are showing their buds
Crocus and daffodil in greeting
And trees are bursting to life in the woods.

Spring has returned once again
Hawthorn is blooming down the lane
The sun is warmer, days are longer
And the farmer sows the grain.

Jean Foster

Shrovetide Fiesta

Ring, ring the Pancake Bell.
To all housewives it will tell
Their pancakes to toss high,
For skipping time is nigh.

Hurry, hurry, to the shore.
Enjoy this custom as of yore.
Ropes across the road to span -
Folk find spaces where they can.

Bright knobbed ropes for tiny tots.
Of clothes line pieces there are lots.
Now the skipping has begun,
Everyone here is having fun.

Mums a-turning keep tight grip.
Jingles repeated as all skip.
Salt, pepper, vinegar, mustard,
Hurry up, you cowardly custard.

One, two three, four,
Hurry, hurry, skip some more.
Five, six, seven, eight.
Come in now or you'll be late.

Helter skelter, helter skelter,
Do not try to run for shelter.
Dolly pepper, dolly pepper, Choice.
Teenagers yell in loudest voice.

In out, in out, some others shout.
That's what Shrovetide's all about.
For skipping fever's gripping
The Foreshore way on Shrovetide Day.

Florence Needler

The Humber Forts

Twin sentinels guard the river mouth
Rusted armour plated towers
Relics of a bygone paranoia
Watching for the promised invasion.

Eroded by tides and sand shifts
Lashed by salt wind and sea spray
They've outlived the necessities of war
We time the tides for a closer look.

Photographs on the unsafe iron walkway
Where *Trespassers will be Prosecuted*
Unaware that these noble proud defenders
Protect England's heart from some lethal strike.

Bull and *Hail Sand* wait on crumbling steel
Enemies long forgotten still to come
They turn their disappointed eyes toward open seas
Ships and sea birds sail by unchallenged.

Ray Waugh

Unemployment

The dusty streets are silent,
No more early morning calls,
No more the cage descends below,
Those dark and blackened walls.

The pit yard, now stands empty
And silent as the night,
What once was full employment,
Was everybody's right.

What is the future, for our youth,
Dole queue or career?
They also want to know the truth,
Is there a job out there.

They work so hard, while still at school,
They try their very best,
With hundreds trying for every post,
This causes most unrest.

There are miners on the dole queue,
Along with men from steel,
It seems a ghost town all around,
The silence is unreal.

Hospitals are closing down,
Old people's home going too,
Where is all this going to end?
We haven't got a clue.

Is no-one going to stop the rot,
Doesn't anybody care,
Will someone listen to our pleas,
Is there anyone out there?

Edna Watford Harvey

Home

Stone walls, stretch for mile upon mile,
Green fields reach up touching heather clad moors.
A river tumbles along over its stony bed,
Overshadowed by rocks so curiously shaped.
Formed by weathers gone past.
Old villages and mills, lonely farmsteads.
Crumbling houses, transformed by the well to do.
Grown, over the centuries, yet strangely unchanging,
For a true dale heart beats on forever.
With each visit comes new enchantment,
New discoveries and old memories lingering from childhood.
My birth place holds my secret dreams.
Nidderdale, Nidderdale, my home, my home.
For here's where my heart is wherever I roam.

Hazel Jackson

Untitled

The War of the Roses blast into my life
On a warm sunny day unaccustomed to strife
Prophetic Pied Piper in destiny's name
Wooed the lost Rose he had come to reclaim
Born of Lancastrian's the salt of the earth
I'd natured the Red Rose our symbol of work
My birthplace was Yorkshire nostalgic the flight
Cause twain were the Counties of Red Rose and White
As I boarded the train on the most fateful day
The reed of the Piper and the tune he did play
Unbeknown to me wasn't a new twist of fate,
But some magical tunes that were sued as a bait
When we left the West and rode Eastwards that day
The Piper he knew I'd return and would stay.

Edith Norris

To Otley Chevin

We love you well, our Chevin hill,
Your beauty is our pride.
In summer's heat or winter's chill
Your vistas are so wide.

We climb your back and to the East -
Sweet villages and plains,
But westward and our eyes do feast
On brooding mountain chains.

This path runs by a darkening wood,
What creatures hide in there?
A world of nature seeks its food
Or makes a secret lair.

From Otley town we daily view
Your changing moods unfold;
From drifting rain to autumn hue,
From snow to sunset gold.

An everlasting bulwark set
In mists of distant time,
You lift our minds above the fret
To thoughts and deeds subline.

Kathleen Padbury

Robin Hood's Bay

Stone steps, uneven cobbles, summer heat,
Shivers in shadows along narrow streets,
Wandering down alleyways and quiet yards
Where pale clematis carelessly falls
Down hand-chiselled herringbone walls.

At the Bay Inn we rest a while on a bench.
Amid chatter and laughter, thirsts to quench,
Still, we sit,
Ale poised between hand and lip.

As gull whitebreasted, soft and smooth as silk,
Webbed feet totter on iron rail,
So close, so close,
We could almost touch her.
She waits alert, patient with watchful eye,
Ever hopeful of easy prey,
Disappointed she wheels away.

To cool pools where sea-birds bathe and sip,
Renewed by freshwater streams that murmur and trip,
Ever-changing, meandering way
Across the beach into the bay.

We gaze over rock shelves stretching out to sea,
Sandy inlets, drifting swirls of steamy heat,
Lost in a moment,
The vision is sweet.

Surrounded by heather moors and golden gorse,
Where the Skylark joyously sings and soars,
Evening clouds gather, the air is still,
As we steal one last glimpse from the brow of a hill.

Christine Lee

Super Tram

Riding along on the Sixty Nine bus,
The roads are busy, everyone's in a rush,
Until we approach the new swimming baths
Where great metal rods, now block the paths,
Huge poles of scaffolding all fixed in place
Steady the traffic to a crawling pace.
Eyes scan the skyline and spot the huge bridge
With it's bevelled edges and blue painted ridge.
What fate is now destined for Sheffield City?
It looks such a mess though it's never been pretty.
Well it's all for a reason, it's not just a scam,
They're preparing the roads for the new Super Tram.

Tricia Mead

My Place

Your moorland hills
fill my awe with wonder
at their timelessness,
snow-covered,
mist-shrouded,
or baked in the sun.

Your serpentine valley
burdens my mind
with its derelict,
forgotten mills,
and the stink from the factories
spewing their chemicals
into the dirty river
that flows by the silent,
and mostly, stagnant canal,
where, once, proud boats
ferried goods to away places.

Your hamlets and villages
you've seen through
countless changes,
and love or despise as I choose,
you are my place,
part of me,
as one day I shall become part of you.

Julia A Smith

An Exile's Dream of Home

I am miles away from my old home,
Where as a child I grew,
the roads and streets I used to roam,
And the parks I played in, too.

I would see the Mansion House again,
And watch the Leger races,
and pray a while to ease the pain
Of unfamiliar places.

Stand by the bridge in Sprotbro' too,
And drive round hair - pin bends,
And see the locks with their lovely view,
The footpaths I would wend.

Oh! why should I live far away?
From all I hold so dear,
I have not seen for many a day,
'Nor shall again, I fear.

To hear once more the dialect,
And see old friends again,
Would they remember? or forget,
and give loneliness and pain.

Perhaps they are all dead and gone,
So unhappy I would be,
I'll sit at home, all alone
And dream that I could see.

My lovely market and High Street,
Where life goes ever faster,
In my mind I'll never beat
My well-loved town, Doncaster.

Kathleen Roelich

Progress

Pop in a chick it's done in a tick.
Throw in your wash go out for a nosh,
The telly adds say it is good!
You're better off with Yorkshire Pudd
Get a car buy a house!
Will you be lucky to keep a spouse?
Get a loan pop in the Bank
Buy yourself a Chieftain tank.
Buy this and get one free.
I've only come in for quarter of tea!

B Lenson

Robin Hood's Bay

Looking out over the North sea menacing and grey
We stood and stared with thoughts so far away.
Cliffs standing defiant against the waves crashing,
seagulls soaring above, calling out with haunting shrilling

The late March sun behind a cloud shyly peeks
lending a warm glow to our frozen cheeks
A breeze caresses our faces and runs through our hair
Feelings sights and sounds for future memories to share

Tasting salt upon our lips as we climbed the steep hill
Atmosphere, tranquillity, nature talking, in the peace and the still
Drinking tea in a small café, a table with a view that's *just so*
capturing the spirit of the bay, framed like a picture in its window.

Little fishing town nestled into the cliffside, homes cling together
as close as the communities they house both now, before and
                                                  forever
Colourful characters tell tales of the good and bad times past
Secret passages, smugglers and brave seamen, legends that will
                                                    last

How do you describe all these things in one line or phrase
How do you express the essence of a place that holds the gaze
You cannot, unless to someone who has been there at least a day
then all you need say is simply, *Remember Robin Hood's Bay.*

David Kennedy

Home Sweet Home

Oh, who would live in Yorkshire
With its hills and so much rain!
Dark skies and muddy puddles;
Will the sun ever shine again?

Stop!
Our hills are our scenery,
Our rain helps us survive!
So, who would live in this greenery?
Me!

Oh, who would live in Yorkshire?
The home might be on a hill!
Rough travel, village shopping,
And a trek to the local mill!

Stop!
What's wrong with feet for transport;
And village trade helps us survive!
So, who would live with this type of sport?
Me!

Denny Rhymer

Where Does Time Go?

Where does time go?
Is it hiding behind the settee,
Or beneath my bed cover?
Does it move too fast
And I too slow?

Searching in despair,
This infinite exploration
Which even Livingstone found elusive
Overwhelms the mere mortal
For time will defeat us all.

Andrew Frith